KIKKOMAN

Oriental Cooking

D0619225

CRESCENT BOOKS

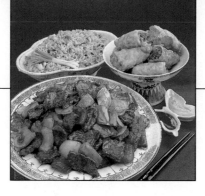

CONTENTS

Copyright © 1989 Kikkoman International Inc.
All rights reserved.

Kikkoman® is a registered trademark owned by Kikkoman
Corporation. The Kikkoman trademark is used in this
cookbook in connection with the following products:

Kikkoman® Soy Sauce
Kikkoman® Lite Soy Sauce
Kikkoman® Teriyaki Sauce
Kikkoman® Teriyaki Baste & Glaze
Kikkoman® Stir-Fry Sauce
Kikkoman® Sweet & Sour Sauce

All recipes developed and tested by the home economists of
the Kikkoman Kitchens.

Library of Congress Catalog Card Number: 89-61697

ISBN 0-517-67596-X

This edition published by:
Crescent Books
Distributed by Outlet Book Company, Inc.
A Random House Company
40 Englehard Ave.
Avenel, New Jersey 07001

Pictured on the front cover: Spring Rolls *(page 11)*, Classic
Chinese Pepper Steak *(page 26)* and New Year Fried Rice
(page 86).

Pictured on the back cover, clockwise from the left:
Japanese Rice Salad *(page 84)*, Crispy Wontons *(page 8)* and
Spicy Chicken *(page 56)*.

Manufactured in USA

h g f e d c b a

KIKKOMAN BRINGS THE ORIENT HOME

Oriental cuisine may be many centuries old, but its distinctive flavors and cooking methods are timeless and well suited for those who have less time to spend in the kitchen. Whether you're an experienced cook or just starting out, you'll enjoy sampling the culinary heritage featured here. This book is filled with delicious, easy-to-prepare recipes—appetizers, main dishes, salads and side dishes—that are perfect for everyday meals and entertaining.

For over 350 years, Asian cooks have relied on the superior quality of naturally brewed Kikkoman Soy Sauce to artfully season their favorite dishes. Kikkoman's six-month brewing process, using only natural ingredients, creates a unique flavor, aroma and color that can't be duplicated.

If you're concerned about the level of sodium in your diet, you'll appreciate Kikkoman Lite Soy Sauce. It has 40 percent less salt, yet retains all the tastiness and aroma of naturally brewed soy sauce because the salt is extracted *after* brewing.

Kikkoman Soy Sauce is the prime ingredient in all of the convenient and tasty sauces featured in these full-flavored recipes. The distinctive flavor of teriyaki is

easy to achieve with Kikkoman Teriyaki Sauce. It's a delicious shortcut to many other Oriental specialties, too. You'll also find Kikkoman Teriyaki Baste & Glaze produces a rich, lush flavor in virtually no time, whether you broil, grill, bake or roast.

Easy-to-use Kikkoman Stir-Fry Sauce, with its authentic flavor, eliminates the fuss of making a stir-fry sauce from scratch. Kikkoman Sweet & Sour Sauce adds just the right amount of traditional Chinese flavor, whether it's used as an ingredient or as a tasty dipping sauce.

Although a variety of familiar cooking techniques are used in preparing Oriental dishes, stir-frying, the most popular technique, is featured throughout this book. Before you begin, take a few minutes to read the following information. Stir-frying is easily mastered, and these helpful guidelines will enhance your enjoyment of these wonderful dishes.

Stir-frying involves the rapid cooking of ingredients in a small amount of oil over high heat for a few minutes. In addition to saving time, the quick cooking preserves the nutrients, flavors, textures and colors of food. Stir-frying can be divided into two separate steps: the preparing of ingredients and the actual cooking.

It is essential to have all the ingredients prepared in advance. This means all cleaning, cutting, measuring, combining, etc. Stir-frying proceeds so quickly that there is no time to do anything else once cooking begins. When cutting meats and vegetables, make the pieces a uniform shape and size to ensure even cooking. Otherwise, one ingredient may overcook while others remain undercooked. To help seal in the natural juices and increase flavor, the meat should be lightly coated with a sauce before cooking.

When you're ready to begin, place a wok or large skillet over high heat. (Preheating the pan prevents the food from sticking.) When a drop of water added to the pan sizzles, the pan is sufficiently hot. Next add the oil, swirling to coat the inside of the pan; heat until the oil is hot, about 30 seconds. Now the ingredients can be added.

Stir-fry the meat first and remove. Then add the vegetables, beginning with those that take the longest to cook. Briskly toss and stir with a flat metal or wooden spatula. Be sure to keep the food in constant motion. This ensures that all surfaces are quickly coated with hot oil to seal in the flavorings, and also to prevent overcooking or burning. To maintain the characteristic Chinese tender-crisp quality, serve stir-fried dishes immediately.

The best oils to use for stir-frying are vegetable oils that can withstand intense heat without smoking. Peanut oil, corn oil and soybean oil are excellent choices.

We hope you enjoy all of the Oriental specialties in this book. Simply follow the recipes closely and you'll be an Oriental chef in virtually no time at all. And, once you've mastered the basics of Oriental cooking, creating your own classics is easy. All you need are quality ingredients, complementary flavors and timely preparation. Don't be afraid to try your own ideas—that's how great chefs are born!

APPETIZERS

MEAT-FILLED ORIENTAL PANCAKES

Makes 2 dozen appetizers

6 Oriental Pancakes (recipe follows)
1 tablespoon cornstarch
3 tablespoons Kikkoman Soy Sauce
1 tablespoon dry sherry
3/4 pound ground beef
1/2 pound ground pork
2/3 cup chopped green onions and tops
1 teaspoon minced fresh ginger root
1 clove garlic, pressed

Prepare Oriental Pancakes on page 8. Combine cornstarch, soy sauce and sherry in large bowl. Add beef pork, green onions, ginger and garlic; mix until thoroughly combined. Spread 1/2 cup meat mixture evenly over each pancake, leaving about a 1/2-inch border on 1 side. Starting with opposite side, roll up pancake jelly-roll fashion. Place rolls, seam side down, in single layer, on heatproof plate; place plate on steamer rack. Set rack in large pot or wok of boiling water. Cover and steam 15 minutes. (For best results, steam all rolls at the same time.) Just before serving, cut rolls diagonally into quarters. Arrange on serving platter and serve hot.

CRISPY WONTONS

Makes 10 appetizer servings

- 3/4 pound ground pork
- 8 water chestnuts, finely chopped
- 1/4 cup finely chopped green onions and tops
- 1 tablespoon Kikkoman Soy Sauce
- 1/2 teaspoon salt
- 1 teaspoon cornstarch
- 1/2 teaspoon grated fresh ginger root
- 1 package (1 lb.) wonton skins
    Vegetable oil for frying
    Tomato catsup and hot mustard *or* Kikkoman Sweet & Sour Sauce

Combine pork, water chestnuts, green onions, soy sauce, salt, cornstarch and ginger in medium bowl; mix well. Place 1/2 teaspoonful pork mixture in center of each wonton skin. Fold wonton skin over filling to form a triangle. Turn top of triangle down to meet fold. Turn over; moisten 1 corner with water. Overlap opposite corner over moistened corner; press firmly. Heat oil in wok or large saucepan over medium-high heat to 375°F. Deep fry wontons, a few at a time, 2 to 3 minutes, or until brown and crispy. Drain on paper towels. Serve warm with catsup and mustard or sweet & sour sauce, as desired.

ORIENTAL PANCAKES:

Beat *4 eggs* in large bowl with wire whisk. Combine *1/2 cup water, 3 tablespoons corn-starch, 2 teaspoons Kikkoman Soy Sauce* and *1/2 teaspoon sugar*; pour into eggs and beat well. Heat an 8-inch omelet or crepe pan over medium heat. Brush bottom of pan with *1/2 teaspoon vegetable oil*; reduce heat to low. Beat egg mixture; pour 1/4 cupful into skillet, lifting and tipping pan from side to side to form a thin round pancake. Cook about 1 to 1 1/2 minutes, or until firm. Carefully lift with spatula and transfer to a sheet of waxed paper. Continue procedure, adding 1/2 teaspoon oil to pan for each pancake. Makes 6 pancakes.

SHRIMP WITH SWEET & SOUR SAUCE

Makes 10 appetizer servings

- 2 pounds medium-size raw shrimp
- 2/3 cup vinegar
- 2/3 cup brown sugar, packed
- 2 teaspoons cornstarch
- 2 tablespoons Kikkoman Soy Sauce
- 1 cup water
- 1/2 teaspoon Tabasco pepper sauce

Peel shrimp, leaving tails on; devein. Simmer in large pot of boiling salted water 5 minutes; drain and cool. Wrap and refrigerate. Combine vinegar, brown sugar, cornstarch, soy sauce and water in small saucepan. Simmer, stirring constantly, until thickened, about 1 minute; stir in pepper sauce. Pour into chafing dish; serve with cold shrimp.

EGG DROP SOUP

Makes about 12 cups

- 3 quarts water
- 9 chicken bouillon cubes
- 1/3 cup Kikkoman Soy Sauce
- 6 eggs, well beaten
- 1 1/2 cups finely chopped green onions and tops

Bring water to boil in large saucepan; add bouillon cubes and stir until dissolved. Stir in soy sauce; return to boil. Remove from heat; add eggs all at once, stirring rapidly in 1 direction with spoon. (Eggs will separate to form fine threads.) Stir in green onions. Serve immediately.

Crispy Wontons

EMPRESS CHICKEN WINGS

Makes 4 to 6 appetizer servings

1 1/2 pounds chicken wings (about
  8 wings)
3 tablespoons Kikkoman Soy Sauce
1 tablespoon dry sherry
1 tablespoon minced fresh ginger root
1 clove garlic, minced
2 tablespoons vegetable oil
1/4 to 1/3 cup cornstarch
2/3 cup water
2 green onions and tops, cut diagonally
  into thin slices
1 teaspoon slivered fresh ginger root

Disjoint chicken wings; discard tips (or save for stock). Combine soy sauce, sherry, minced ginger and garlic in large bowl; stir in chicken. Cover and refrigerate 1 hour, stirring occasionally. Remove chicken; reserve marinade. Heat oil in large skillet over medium heat. Lightly coat chicken pieces with cornstarch; add to skillet and brown slowly on all sides. Remove chicken; drain off fat. Stir water and reserved marinade into same skillet. Add chicken; sprinkle green onions and slivered ginger evenly over chicken. Cover and simmer 5 minutes, or until chicken is tender.

Empress Chicken Wings

SPRING ROLLS

Makes 8 appetizer servings

- 1/2 pound ground pork
- 1 teaspoon Kikkoman Soy Sauce
- 1 teaspoon dry sherry
- 1/2 teaspoon garlic salt
- 2 tablespoons vegetable oil
- 3 cups fresh bean sprouts
- 1/2 cup sliced onion
- 1 tablespoon Kikkoman Soy Sauce
- 1 tablespoon cornstarch
- 3/4 cup water, divided
- 8 sheets egg roll skins
- 1/2 cup prepared biscuit mix
- 1 egg, beaten
  - Vegetable oil for frying
  - Hot mustard, tomato catsup and Kikkoman Soy Sauce

Combine pork, 1 teaspoon soy sauce, sherry and garlic salt; mix well. Let stand 15 minutes. Heat 2 tablespoons oil in hot wok or large skillet over medium-high heat; brown pork mixture in hot oil. Add bean sprouts, onion and 1 tablespoon soy sauce. Stir-fry until vegetables are tender-crisp; drain and cool. Dissolve cornstarch in 1/4 cup water. Place about 1/3 cupful pork mixture on lower half of egg roll skin. Moisten left and right edges with cornstarch mixture. Fold bottom edge up to just cover filling. Fold left and right edges 1/2 inch over; roll up jelly-roll fashion. Moisten top edge with cornstarch mixture and seal. Complete all rolls. Combine biscuit mix, egg and remaining 1/2 cup water in small bowl; dip each roll in batter. Heat oil for frying in wok or large saucepan over medium-high heat to 370°F. Deep fry rolls, a few at a time, in hot oil 5 to 7 minutes, or until golden brown, turning often. Drain on paper towels. Slice each roll in half. Serve with mustard, catsup and soy sauce as desired.

SHRIMP TERIYAKI

Makes 10 appetizer servings

- 1/2 cup Kikkoman Soy Sauce
- 2 tablespoons sugar
- 1 tablespoon vegetable oil
- 1 1/2 teaspoons cornstarch
- 1 clove garlic, crushed
- 1 teaspoon minced fresh ginger root
- 2 tablespoons water
- 2 pounds medium-size raw shrimp, peeled and deveined

Blend soy sauce, sugar, oil, cornstarch, garlic, ginger and water in small saucepan. Simmer, stirring constantly, until thickened, about 1 minute; cool. Coat shrimp with sauce; drain off excess. Place on rack of broiler pan. Broil 5 inches from heat source 3 to 4 minutes on each side, or until shrimp are opaque and cooked. Serve immediately with wooden picks.

FRESH PINEAPPLE WITH SESAME DIP

Makes about 6 appetizer servings

- 2 tablespoons sesame seed, toasted
- 1 package (8 oz.) cream cheese, softened
- 1 tablespoon Kikkoman Soy Sauce
- 1/4 teaspoon Tabasco pepper sauce
- 6 tablespoons water
- 1 fresh pineapple

Crush sesame seed in blender at high speed. Add cream cheese, soy sauce, pepper sauce and water; blend well. Turn into serving bowl; set aside. Cut a thick slice from both top and bottom of pineapple; discard. Peel and remove "eyes." Cut lengthwise into 8 strips; remove core. Cut each strip crosswise into thirds; cut each third lengthwise into 3 bite-size pieces. Serve with sesame dip.

CANTONESE MEATBALLS

Makes 6 to 8 appetizer servings

- 1 can (20 oz.) pineapple chunks in syrup
- 3 tablespoons brown sugar, packed
- 5 tablespoons Kikkoman Teriyaki Sauce, divided
- 1 tablespoon vinegar
- 1 tablespoon tomato catsup
- 1 pound lean ground beef
- 2 tablespoons instant minced onion
- 2 tablespoons cornstarch
- 1/4 cup water

Drain pineapple; reserve syrup. Combine syrup, brown sugar, 3 tablespoons teriyaki sauce, vinegar and catsup; set aside. Mix beef with remaining 2 tablespoons teriyaki sauce and onion; shape into 20 meatballs. Brown meatballs in large skillet; drain off excess fat. Pour syrup mixture over meatballs; simmer 10 minutes, stirring occasionally. Dissolve cornstarch in water; stir into skillet with pineapple. Cook and stir until sauce thickens and pineapple is heated through.

YAKITORI

Makes 4 dozen appetizers

- 3 pounds chicken breasts
- 1 bunch green onions, cut into 1-inch lengths
- 1 pound chicken livers, trimmed, rinsed and drained
- 1 cup Kikkoman Soy Sauce
- 1/4 cup sugar
- 1 tablespoon vegetable oil
- 2 cloves garlic, pressed
- 3/4 teaspoon ground ginger

Remove skin and bones from chicken, keeping meat in 1 piece; cut into 1-inch lengths. Thread chicken pieces onto metal or bamboo skewers with green onions (spear through side) and chicken livers. Arrange skewers in large shallow pan. Blend soy sauce, sugar, oil, garlic and ginger; pour mixture over skewers. Brush each skewer thoroughly with sauce. Cover and refrigerate about 1 hour, turning skewers over occasionally. Reserving marinade, remove skewers and place on rack of broiler pan. Broil 5 inches from heat source 3 minutes on each side, or until chicken is tender; brush with reserved marinade after turning.

ORIENTAL DRIED BEEF STRIPS

Makes about 2 dozen strips

- 2 pounds beef flank steak
- 1/2 cup Kikkoman Soy Sauce
- 1/4 teaspoon garlic powder
- 1/8 teaspoon pepper

Trim all visible fat from steak. Cut steak lengthwise, along grain, into long, 1/4-inch-wide strips; place in large bowl. Combine soy sauce, garlic powder and pepper. Pour over beef strips; toss to coat well. Arrange strips, in single layer, being careful not to overlap, on 1 or 2 racks placed on large baking sheet. Bake at 175°F. to 200°F. 10 to 12 hours, or until thoroughly dry. Store at room temperature in airtight containers or in plastic bags.

Clear Japanese Soup with Sesame Cheese Crackers

SESAME CHEESE CRACKERS

Makes 8 appetizer servings

    1 cup all-purpose flour
   1/2 teaspoon salt
   1/8 teaspoon ground red pepper (cayenne)
    6 tablespoons cold butter or margarine
    1 cup (4 oz.) finely grated Cheddar cheese
   1/4 cup sesame seed, toasted
   1/2 teaspoon Kikkoman Soy Sauce
   4 1/2 to 7 1/2 teaspoons ice-cold water

Combine flour, salt and pepper in medium bowl; cut in butter until mixture resembles coarse crumbs. Stir in cheese and sesame seed. Combine soy sauce and 3 teaspoons water; stir into dry ingredients. Add more water, a little at a time, mixing lightly until dough begins to stick together. Turn out dough and press together on lightly floured board or pastry cloth; roll out to 1/8-inch thickness. Cut dough into 2 × 1-inch rectangles with pastry wheel or knife. Place on lightly greased baking sheets and bake at 400°F. 8 to 10 minutes, or until lightly browned. Remove crackers to rack to cool.

CLEAR JAPANESE SOUP

Makes about 6 cups

   1 1/2 quarts chicken broth
    1/3 cup dry sherry
   4 1/2 teaspoons Kikkoman Soy Sauce
      1 lemon, thinly sliced
Garnishes:
      5 to 6 fresh mushrooms, sliced
      2 green onions and tops, sliced
        diagonally
      1 carrot, very thinly sliced

Bring broth to simmer in large saucepan. Add sherry and soy sauce; simmer 2 to 3 minutes. Ladle soup into small bowls; float a lemon slice in each bowl. Arrange garnishes on tray and add to soup as desired.

PRAWNS-IN-SHELL

Makes 8 appetizer servings

- 1 pound large raw prawns
- 2 tablespoons dry white wine, divided
- 1/2 teaspoon grated fresh ginger root
- 1/4 cup vegetable oil
- 2 tablespoons coarsely chopped green onions and tops
- 1 teaspoon coarsely chopped fresh ginger root
- 1 clove garlic, chopped
- 2 small red chili peppers,* coarsely chopped
- 1 tablespoon sugar
- 3 tablespoons tomato catsup
- 2 tablespoons Kikkoman Soy Sauce
- 1/2 teaspoon cornstarch

Wash and devein prawns; do not peel. Cut prawns diagonally into halves; place in medium bowl. Sprinkle 1 tablespoon wine and grated ginger over prawns. Heat oil in hot wok or large skillet over high heat. Add prawns; stir-fry until completely pink or red. Add green onions, chopped ginger, garlic and chili peppers; stir-fry only until onions are tender. Combine sugar, catsup, soy sauce, remaining 1 tablespoon wine and cornstarch; pour into pan. Cook and stir until sauce boils and thickens. Serve immediately. Garnish as desired.

*Wear rubber gloves when working with chilis and wash hands in warm soapy water. Avoid touching face or eyes.

TERIYAKI LAMB RIBLETS

Makes 8 appetizer servings

- 3 pounds lamb breast riblets, cut into serving-size pieces
- 1/3 cup Kikkoman Teriyaki Sauce

Place riblets in large saucepan; add enough water to cover and bring to boil. Reduce heat; simmer, covered, 20 minutes. Remove riblets from saucepan; cool. Pat dry with paper towel to remove excess water. Place riblets on rack of broiler pan; brush thoroughly with teriyaki sauce. Broil riblets about 4 inches from heat source 4 minutes on each side, brushing frequently with teriyaki sauce.

SESAME PORK TIDBITS WITH SWEET & SOUR SAUCE

Makes about 3 dozen appetizers

- 1 1/2 pounds boneless pork loin
- 1/2 cup cornstarch
- 1/4 cup Kikkoman Teriyaki Sauce
- 3 tablespoons sesame seed, lightly toasted
- Sweet & Sour Sauce (recipe follows)
- 3 cups vegetable oil

Trim excess fat from pork; cut into 1-inch cubes and set aside. Thoroughly combine cornstarch, teriyaki sauce and sesame seed in medium bowl (mixture will be very stiff). Stir in pork cubes; let stand 30 minutes. Meanwhile, prepare Sweet & Sour Sauce; keep warm. Heat oil in medium saucepan over medium-high heat to 300°F. Add 1/3 of the pork cubes and cook, stirring constantly, until golden brown, about 2 minutes. Remove and drain thoroughly on paper towels. Repeat with remaining pork. Serve immediately with warm Sweet & Sour Sauce.

SWEET & SOUR SAUCE:
Combine *1/4 cup sugar, 1/4 cup vinegar, 1/4 cup catsup, 1/4 cup water, 1 tablespoon Kikkoman Teriyaki Sauce* and *1 1/2 teaspoons cornstarch* in small saucepan. Cook over high heat, stirring constantly, until thickened.

Prawns-in-Shell

STEAMED STUFFED ZUCCHINI ROUNDS

Makes 6 to 8 appetizer servings

4 zucchini, 6 to 7 inches long, about
    1 1/2 inches in diameter
1/2 cup Kikkoman Teriyaki Sauce
1/2 pound ground beef
1/2 cup dry bread crumbs
1/4 cup minced green onions and tops

Trim off and discard ends of zucchini; cut crosswise into 3/4-inch lengths. Scoop out flesh, leaving about 1/8-inch shell on sides and bottoms; reserve flesh. Place zucchini rounds in large plastic bag; pour in teriyaki sauce. Press air out of bag; tie top securely. Marinate 30 minutes, turning bag over occasionally. Meanwhile, coarsely chop zucchini flesh; reserve 1/2 cup. Remove zucchini rounds from marinade; reserve 1/4 cup marinade. Combine reserved marinade with beef, bread crumbs, green onions and 1/2 cup reserved zucchini flesh. Fill each round with about 2 teaspoonfuls beef mixture. Place rounds, filled side up, on steamer rack. Set rack in large pot or wok of boiling water. (Do not allow water level to reach zucchini.) Cover and steam 6 minutes, or until zucchini rounds are tender-crisp when pierced with fork. Serve immediately.

WAIKIKI APPETIZERS

Makes 6 to 8 appetizer servings

1 1/2 pounds bulk pork sausage
   1 can (20 oz.) pineapple chunks in syrup
1/2 cup brown sugar, packed
1/4 cup lemon juice
   2 tablespoons cornstarch
   2 tablespoons Kikkoman Soy Sauce
1/2 cup chopped green pepper
1/2 cup drained maraschino cherries

Shape sausage into 1/2- to 3/4-inch balls. Place in single layer in baking pan. Bake in 400°F. oven 25 minutes, or until cooked; drain on paper towels. Meanwhile, drain pineapple; reserve syrup. Add enough water to syrup to measure 1 cup; combine with brown sugar, lemon juice, cornstarch and soy sauce in large saucepan. Cook and stir until sauce boils and thickens. Fold in green pepper, cherries, pineapple chunks and drained cooked sausage. To serve, turn into chafing dish.

TOASTED SESAME CHEESE SPREAD

Makes 4 to 6 appetizer servings

2 tablespoons Kikkoman Soy Sauce
1 package (3 oz.) cream cheese
4 teaspoons sesame seed, toasted
   Assorted crackers

Pour soy sauce over cream cheese block in small dish, turning over several times to coat all sides. Cover; refrigerate 2 hours, turning cheese block over often. Remove cheese block from soy sauce and roll in sesame seed. Refrigerate until ready to serve with crackers.

Top: Steamed Stuffed Zucchini Rounds
Bottom: Waikiki Appetizers

HOT & SOUR SOUP

Makes about 5 cups

- 1 can (10½ oz.) condensed chicken broth
- 2 soup cans water
- 1 can (4 oz.) sliced mushrooms
- 2 tablespoons cornstarch
- 2 tablespoons Kikkoman Soy Sauce
- 2 tablespoons distilled white vinegar
- ½ teaspoon Tabasco pepper sauce
- 1 egg, beaten
- 2 green onions and tops, chopped

Combine chicken broth, water, mushrooms, cornstarch, soy sauce, vinegar and pepper sauce in medium saucepan. Bring to boil over high heat, stirring constantly, until slightly thickened. Gradually pour egg into boiling soup, stirring constantly in 1 direction. Remove from heat; stir in green onions. Garnish with additional chopped green onions or cilantro, as desired. Serve immediately.

BITS O' TERIYAKI CHICKEN

Makes 6 appetizer servings

- ½ cup Kikkoman Teriyaki Sauce
- 1 teaspoon sugar
- 2 whole chicken breasts, skinned and boned
- 1 teaspoon cornstarch
- 1 tablespoon water
- 1 tablespoon vegetable oil
- 2 tablespoons sesame seed, toasted

Combine teriyaki sauce and sugar in small bowl. Cut chicken into 1-inch pieces; stir into teriyaki sauce mixture. Marinate 30 minutes, stirring occasionally. Remove chicken; reserve 2 tablespoons marinade. Combine reserved marinade, cornstarch and water in small bowl; set aside. Heat oil in hot wok or large skillet over medium-high heat. Add chicken and sesame seed; stir-fry 2 minutes. Stir in cornstarch mixture. Cook and stir until mixture boils and thickens and chicken is tender, about 1 minute. Turn into chafing dish or onto serving platter. Serve warm with wooden picks.

Hot & Sour Soup

POLYNESIAN KABOBS

Makes 25 appetizers

1 can (20 oz.) pineapple chunks in syrup
6 tablespoons Kikkoman Soy Sauce
3 tablespoons honey
1 tablespoon dry sherry
1 teaspoon grated orange peel
1/8 teaspoon garlic powder
2 pounds cooked ham, cut into 25 cubes
    (1 inch)
1 pound thickly sliced bacon
25 large stuffed olives
25 cherry tomatoes

Drain pineapple; reserve syrup. Blend syrup, soy sauce, honey, sherry, orange peel and garlic powder in large bowl; stir in ham cubes. Cover; refrigerate 1 hour, stirring occasionally. Cut each bacon slice crosswise in half; wrap pineapple chunks with halved bacon slices. Thread bamboo or metal skewers with a wrapped pineapple chunk, an olive, another wrapped pineapple, a marinated ham cube and a cherry tomato. Place skewers on rack of broiler pan; brush with marinade. Broil 3 to 4 inches from heat source 2 to 3 minutes on each side, or until bacon is crisp.

BEEF AND FRUIT SKEWERS

Makes 2 dozen appetizers

1 can (20 oz.) pineapple chunks in syrup
1/2 cup Kikkoman Soy Sauce
1 tablespoon cornstarch
2 cloves garlic, pressed
2 teaspoons minced crystallized ginger
1 1/2 pounds boneless beef sirloin, about
    1/2 inch thick
1 package (12 oz.) pitted prunes
1 bunch green onions, cut into 1-inch
    lengths
2 dozen drained maraschino cherries
    (optional)

Drain pineapple; reserve syrup. Blend syrup, soy sauce, cornstarch, garlic and ginger in small saucepan. Cook and stir until sauce thickens; cool. Meanwhile, cut beef into 1-inch pieces. Thread beef onto bamboo or metal skewers alternately with pineapple chunks, prunes and green onions (spear through side), ending with cherries. Dip into sauce, brushing to thoroughly coat meat and fruit; drain slightly. Place skewers on rack of broiler pan. Broil to desired degree of doneness, turning once and brushing with sauce.

GARLIC CHICKEN BUNDLES

Makes 8 to 10 appetizer servings

2¼ pounds chicken breasts, skinned and
  boned
4 tablespoons Kikkoman Soy Sauce,
  divided
5½ teaspoons cornstarch, divided
4 teaspoons minced garlic, divided
¾ teaspoon sugar
⅓ cup water
2 tablespoons vegetable oil, divided
1 cup diced carrot
½ cup chopped green onions and tops
¼ cup chopped toasted almonds
1 tablespoon minced fresh cilantro or
  parsley
8 to 10 butter or iceberg lettuce leaves

Cut chicken into ½-inch pieces. Combine 3 tablespoons soy sauce, 4½ teaspoons cornstarch, 3 teaspoons garlic and sugar in small bowl; stir in chicken. Let stand 15 minutes. Meanwhile, combine water, remaining 1 tablespoon soy sauce and 1 teaspoon cornstarch; set aside. Heat 1 tablespoon oil in hot wok or large skillet over high heat. Add chicken and stir-fry 4 minutes; remove. Heat remaining 1 tablespoon oil in same pan. Add carrot and remaining 1 teaspoon garlic; stir-fry 1 minute. Add green onions; stir-fry 1 minute longer. Stir in chicken and soy sauce mixture. Cook and stir until mixture boils and thickens. Remove from heat and stir in almonds and cilantro. To serve, fill each lettuce leaf with about ¼ cup chicken mixture. If desired, fold lettuce around filling to enclose.

Garlic Chicken Bundles

Glazed Ginger Chicken

GLAZED GINGER CHICKEN

Makes 8 appetizer servings

1 tablespoon sesame seed, toasted
1 tablespoon cornstarch
5 tablespoons Kikkoman Soy Sauce
3 tablespoons plum jam
1 tablespoon minced fresh ginger root
1 clove garlic, pressed
8 small chicken thighs (about 2 pounds)

Cut eight 8-inch squares of aluminum foil; set aside. Combine sesame seed, cornstarch, soy sauce, plum jam, ginger and garlic in small saucepan. Bring to boil over medium heat, stirring constantly. Remove from heat and cool slightly. Stir in thighs, a few at a time, to coat each piece well. Place 1 thigh, skin side up, on each foil square. Divide and spoon remaining sauce evenly over thighs. Fold ends of foil to form a package; crease and fold down to secure well. Place foil bundles, seam side up, in single layer, on steamer rack. Set rack in large pot or wok of boiling water. (Do not allow water level to reach bundles.) Cover and steam 30 minutes, or until chicken is tender. Garnish as desired. Serve immediately.

SPICY PORK STRIPS

Makes 6 to 8 appetizer servings

1 pound boneless pork chops, 1/2 inch thick
1/3 cup Kikkoman Soy Sauce
1/4 cup minced green onions and tops
1 tablespoon sugar
1 tablespoon sesame seed, toasted
3 tablespoons water
1 1/2 teaspoons minced fresh ginger root
1 teaspoon Tabasco pepper sauce
1 clove garlic, minced

Slice pork into 1/4-inch-thick strips, about 4 inches long. Thread onto metal or bamboo skewers, keeping meat as flat as possible. Arrange skewers in large shallow pan. Blend soy sauce, green onions, sugar, sesame seed, water, ginger, pepper sauce and garlic, stirring until sugar dissolves. Pour mixture evenly over skewers; turn over to coat all sides. Let stand 30 minutes, turning skewers over occasionally. Reserving marinade, remove skewers and place on rack of broiler pan; brush with reserved marinade. Broil 3 minutes, or until pork is tender, turning once and basting with additional marinade.

SAUCY SHRIMP

Makes 6 appetizer servings

1/2 pound medium-size raw shrimp
1/4 cup Kikkoman Teriyaki Baste & Glaze
2 tablespoons dry sherry
1 tablespoon lime juice
1 tablespoon sliced green onions and tops
3 to 4 drops Tabasco pepper sauce

Peel, devein and butterfly shrimp. Combine teriyaki baste & glaze, sherry, lime juice, green onions and pepper sauce in medium bowl; stir in shrimp. Cover; refrigerate at least 1 hour, stirring occasionally. Remove shrimp and place on rack of broiler pan. Broil 2 to 3 minutes on each side, or until shrimp are opaque and cooked. Serve immediately with wooden picks.

BEEF KUSHISASHI

Makes 10 to 12 appetizer servings

1/2 cup Kikkoman Soy Sauce
1/4 cup chopped green onions and tops
2 tablespoons sugar
1 tablespoon vegetable oil
1 1/2 teaspoons cornstarch
1 clove garlic, pressed
1 teaspoon grated fresh ginger root
2 1/2 pounds boneless beef sirloin steak

Blend soy sauce, green onions, sugar, oil, cornstarch, garlic and ginger in small saucepan. Simmer, stirring constantly, until thickened, about 1 minute; cool. Cover and set aside. Slice beef into 1/8-inch-thick strips about 4 inches long and 1 inch wide. Thread onto bamboo or metal skewers keeping meat as flat as possible; brush both sides of beef with sauce. Place skewers on rack of broiler pan; broil to desired degree of doneness.

MARINATED MUSHROOMS

Makes 4 appetizer servings

1/4 cup distilled white vinegar
1 tablespoon sugar
2 teaspoons Kikkoman Soy Sauce
1 tablespoon water
1 can (4 oz.) whole mushrooms, drained
Toasted sesame seed (optional)

Thoroughly combine vinegar, sugar, soy sauce and water in small bowl. Add mushrooms and toss to coat; sprinkle with sesame seed. Marinate 45 to 60 minutes, stirring occasionally. Drain off marinade; serve mushrooms with wooden picks.

Top: Spicy Pork Strips
Bottom: Beef Kushisashi

PARCHMENT-WRAPPED CHICKEN

Makes 8 appetizer servings

2 whole chicken breasts, skinned and boned
3 tablespoons Kikkoman Soy Sauce
1 teaspoon ginger juice*
1/4 teaspoon sugar
  Boiling water
1/2 pound fresh bean sprouts
6 green onions and tops, cut into 2-inch lengths and slivered
1/3 cup chopped toasted walnuts

Cut eight 8-inch squares of parchment paper; set aside. Cut chicken into thin, narrow strips, about 3 inches long. Combine soy sauce, ginger juice and sugar in large bowl; stir in chicken. Let stand 30 minutes. Meanwhile, pour boiling water over bean sprouts; let stand 1 minute. Drain; cool under cold water and drain well. Thoroughly toss chicken mixture with bean sprouts, green onions and walnuts. Place about 1/2 cupful chicken mixture in center of each parchment square. Fold bottom point of parchment over filling; crease just below filling and fold point over and under filling. Fold side points over filling, overlapping slightly. Crease paper to hold folds. Fold remaining corner down so point extends below bottom of bundle; tuck this point between folded sides. Crease paper to hold folds. Repeat with remaining parchment squares. Place bundles, seam side down, in single layer, on steamer rack. Set rack in large pot or wok of boiling water. (Do not allow water level to reach bundles.) Cover and steam about 7 minutes, or until chicken is tender. Serve immediately.

*Peel fresh ginger root, then squeeze through garlic press.

EGG FLOWER SOUP WITH CORN

Makes about 4 1/2 cups

1 can (10 1/2 oz.) condensed chicken broth
2 soup cans water
2 slices fresh ginger root, each 1/4 inch thick
2 tablespoons plus 2 teaspoons cornstarch
1/4 cup water
1/2 cup whole kernel corn
1 egg, beaten
2 tablespoons chopped green onions and tops
4 teaspoons Kikkoman Soy Sauce

Combine chicken broth, 2 soup cans water and ginger in medium saucepan. Bring to boil over high heat; reduce heat, cover and simmer 5 minutes. Discard ginger. Combine cornstarch and 1/4 cup water; stir into saucepan with corn. Cook over high heat, stirring constantly, until mixture boils and is slightly thickened. Gradually pour egg into boiling soup, stirring constantly, but gently, in 1 direction. Remove from heat; stir in green onions and soy sauce. Serve immediately.

MONGOLIAN ALMONDS

Makes 1 cup

1 cup whole natural almonds
2 tablespoons Kikkoman Teriyaki Sauce
1 teaspoon brown sugar
1/8 to 1/4 teaspoon Tabasco pepper sauce
1 tablespoon water
1/2 teaspoon vegetable oil

Toast almonds on ungreased baking sheet in preheated 350°F. oven 10 minutes without stirring. Remove pan from oven and cool almonds in pan on wire rack. *Reduce oven temperature to 250°F.* Combine teriyaki sauce, brown sugar, pepper sauce and water in narrow 1-quart saucepan. Bring to boil over medium-low heat. Stir in almonds and boil about 5 minutes, or until sauce is absorbed by almonds, stirring frequently. Add oil and toss almonds until coated; turn out onto baking sheet, separating almonds. Bake 5 minutes; stir and turn almonds over. Bake 5 minutes longer. Remove from pan to large plate; cool in single layer. Store in loose-fitting container or plastic bag.

PAGODA CHICKEN WINGS

Makes 4 to 6 appetizer servings

1³/₄ pounds chicken wings (about 10 wings)
  ¹/₂ cup Kikkoman Soy Sauce
  ¹/₄ cup honey
  1 tablespoon sesame seed, toasted
  1 clove garlic, minced
  1 teaspoon ground ginger
  1 teaspoon ground cinnamon
  ¹/₄ teaspoon ground cloves
  ¹/₄ teaspoon anise seed, crushed
  ¹/₄ teaspoon fennel seed, crushed

Place chicken in large plastic bag. Combine soy sauce, honey, sesame seed, garlic, ginger, cinnamon, cloves, anise and fennel; pour over chicken. Press air out of bag; tie top securely. Turn over several times to coat pieces well. Refrigerate 2 to 4 hours, turning bag over occasionally. Reserving marinade, remove chicken and place on rack of broiler pan. Broil 4 inches from heat source 5 minutes. Turn pieces over and baste with reserved marinade. Broil 5 minutes longer, or until chicken is tender, basting occasionally with remaining marinade.

KOREAN BEEF STICKS

Makes 6 to 8 appetizer servings

  1 pound boneless beef sirloin steak, about ¹/₂ inch thick
  ¹/₄ cup Kikkoman Soy Sauce
  1 tablespoon sesame seed, toasted
  1 tablespoon water
  2 teaspoons sugar
  ¹/₂ teaspoon Tabasco pepper sauce
  1 clove garlic, pressed

MICROWAVE DIRECTIONS:

Slice beef into ¹/₄-inch-thick strips, each about 4 to 5 inches long. Thread onto bamboo skewers, keeping meat as flat as possible. Arrange skewers in large shallow pan. Blend soy sauce, sesame seed, water, sugar, pepper sauce and garlic, stirring until sugar dissolves. Pour mixture evenly over skewers; turn over to coat all sides. Let stand 30 minutes, turning skewers over occasionally. Remove skewers from marinade; place half on flat, microwave-safe plate. Microwave on High 30 seconds. Turn skewers over and bring skewers from outside of plate to center. Microwave on High 30 seconds (for rare), or to desired degree of doneness. Repeat procedure with remaining skewers.

Pagoda Chicken Wings

BEEF

CLASSIC CHINESE PEPPER STEAK

Makes 4 servings

- 1 pound boneless beef sirloin steak
- 1 tablespoon Kikkoman Stir-Fry Sauce
- 2 tablespoons vegetable oil, divided
- 2 medium-size green, red or yellow bell peppers, cut into 1-inch squares
- 2 medium onions, cut into 1-inch squares
- 1/4 cup Kikkoman Stir-Fry Sauce
  Hot cooked rice (optional)

Cut beef across grain into thin strips, then into 1-inch squares; coat with 1 tablespoon stir-fry sauce. Heat 1 tablespoon oil in hot wok or large skillet over high heat. Add beef and stir-fry 1 minute; remove. Heat remaining 1 tablespoon oil in same pan. Add peppers and onions; stir-fry 5 minutes. Stir in beef and 1/4 cup stir-fry sauce; cook and stir just until beef and vegetables are coated with sauce. Serve immediately with rice.

DRAGON BEEF KABOBS

Makes 4 servings

1¼ pounds boneless beef sirloin steak,
    1½ inches thick
¼ cup Kikkoman Teriyaki Sauce
1 tablespoon peanut butter
1 teaspoon brown sugar
1 teaspoon garlic powder
½ teaspoon Tabasco pepper sauce
1 can (8¼ oz.) pineapple chunks,
    drained

MICROWAVE DIRECTIONS:

Cut beef into 1½-inch cubes; place in medium bowl. Blend teriyaki sauce, peanut butter, brown sugar, garlic powder and pepper sauce. Pour mixture over beef, turning pieces over to coat thoroughly. Marinate 1 hour, turning pieces over occasionally. Reserving marinade, remove beef and thread alternately with pineapple chunks on 4 wooden or bamboo skewers. Arrange skewers in single layer on 12-inch round microwave-safe platter. Brush with reserved marinade. Microwave on High 2 minutes. Turn skewers over and rotate positions on platter, moving center skewers to edge. Brush with marinade. Microwave on High 2 minutes longer, or to desired degree of doneness.

YANGTZE STIR-FRY

Makes 2 to 3 servings

½ pound boneless tender beef steak
    (sirloin, rib eye or top loin)
4 tablespoons Kikkoman Stir-Fry Sauce,
    divided
1 pound Swiss chard or romaine lettuce
2 tablespoons vegetable oil, divided
1 medium onion, cut into ½-inch strips
⅛ to ¼ teaspoon crushed red pepper
⅛ teaspoon salt
½ cup unsalted roasted peanuts

Cut beef across grain into thin slices. Coat with 1 tablespoon stir-fry sauce; let stand 10 minutes. Separate and rinse chard; pat dry. Cut leaves crosswise into 1-inch strips, separating stems from leaves. Heat 1 tablespoon oil in hot wok or large skillet over high heat. Add beef and stir-fry 1 minute; remove. Heat remaining 1 tablespoon oil in same pan. Add chard stems, onion and red pepper. Sprinkle with salt and stir-fry 4 minutes. Add chard leaves; stir-fry 2 minutes. Add beef and remaining 3 tablespoons stir-fry sauce; cook and stir until vegetables are coated with sauce. Remove from heat; stir in peanuts.

SICHUAN BEEF & SNOW PEAS

Makes 2 to 3 servings

½ pound boneless tender beef steak
    (sirloin, rib eye or top loin)
2 tablespoons cornstarch, divided
3 tablespoons Kikkoman Soy Sauce,
    divided
1 tablespoon dry sherry
1 clove garlic, minced
¾ cup water
¼ to ½ teaspoon crushed red pepper
2 tablespoons vegetable oil, divided
6 ounces fresh snow peas, trimmed
1 medium onion, chunked
    Salt
1 medium tomato, chunked
    Hot cooked rice

Slice beef across grain into thin strips. Combine 1 tablespoon *each* cornstarch and soy sauce with sherry and garlic in small bowl; stir in beef. Let stand 15 minutes. Meanwhile, combine water, remaining 1 tablespoon cornstarch, 2 tablespoons soy sauce and red pepper; set aside. Heat 1 tablespoon oil in hot wok or large skillet over high heat. Add beef and stir-fry 1 minute; remove. Heat remaining 1 tablespoon oil in same pan. Add snow peas and onion; lightly sprinkle with salt and stir-fry 3 minutes. Add beef, soy sauce mixture and tomato. Cook and stir until sauce boils and thickens and tomato is heated through. Serve immediately with rice.

Sichuan Beef & Snow Peas

BEEF & NAPA WITH NOODLES

Makes 4 servings

1 small head napa (Chinese cabbage)
  Boiling water
½ pound boneless tender beef steak
  (sirloin, rib eye or top loin)
6 tablespoons Kikkoman Stir-Fry Sauce,
  divided
⅛ to ¼ teaspoon crushed red pepper
2 tablespoons vegetable oil, divided
¼ pound green onions, cut into 2-inch
  lengths, separating whites from tops
1 large red bell pepper, cut into strips
  Hot cooked vermicelli or thin spaghetti

Separate and rinse napa; pat dry. Thinly slice enough leaves crosswise to measure 8 cups; place in colander or large strainer. Pour boiling water over cabbage just until leaves wilt. Cool under cold water; drain thoroughly. Cut beef across grain into thin slices, then into strips. Combine 1 tablespoon stir-fry sauce and crushed red pepper in small bowl; stir in beef to coat. Heat 1 tablespoon oil in hot wok or large skillet over high heat. Add beef and stir-fry 1 minute; remove. Heat remaining 1 table-spoon oil in same pan; add white parts of green onions and stir-fry 1 minute. Add red bell pepper; stir-fry 2 minutes. Add green onion tops; stir-fry 2 minutes longer. Add beef, cabbage and remaining 5 tablespoons stir-fry sauce; cook and stir until vegetables are coated with sauce. Serve immediately over vermicelli.

Beef & Napa with Noodles

SICHUAN BEEF STEW

Makes 6 servings

- 2 pounds boneless beef chuck
- 2 cloves garlic, pressed
- 4 tablespoons Kikkoman Soy Sauce, divided
- 3 teaspoons sugar, divided
- 1 cup water
- 1/2 to 3/4 teaspoon crushed red pepper
- 3/4 teaspoon fennel seed, crushed
- 1/4 teaspoon black pepper
- 1/4 teaspoon ground cloves
- 1/4 teaspoon ground ginger
- 1 tablespoon vegetable oil
- 2 tablespoons cornstarch
- 2 tablespoons water

Cut beef into 2-inch cubes. Combine garlic, 2 tablespoons soy sauce and 1 teaspoon sugar in large bowl; stir in beef cubes until well coated. Let stand 15 minutes. Meanwhile, combine 1 cup water, remaining 2 tablespoons soy sauce, 2 teaspoons sugar, red pepper, fennel, black pepper, cloves and ginger; set aside. Heat oil in Dutch oven or large skillet over high heat. Brown beef on all sides in hot oil. Stir in soy sauce mixture. Bring to boil; reduce heat and simmer, covered, 2 hours, or until beef is very tender. Combine cornstarch with 2 tablespoons water; stir into beef mixture. Cook and stir until mixture boils and thickens, about 1 minute.

MANDARIN ORANGE BEEF

Makes 4 servings

- 1 pound boneless tender beef steak (sirloin, rib eye or top loin)
- 2 tablespoons vegetable oil
- 3 green onions, cut into 2-inch lengths, separating whites from tops
- 1/4 cup Kikkoman Stir-Fry Sauce
- 1 can (11 oz.) mandarin orange segments, drained

Cut beef across grain into thin slices, then into strips. Heat oil in hot wok or large skillet over high heat. Add beef; stir-fry 1 minute. Add white parts of green onions; stir-fry 1 minute. Add green onion tops; stir-fry 1 minute. Add stir-fry sauce and oranges; cook and stir only until heated through.

FIERY BEEF STIR-FRY

Makes 2 to 3 servings

- 1/2 pound boneless tender beef steak (sirloin, rib eye or top loin)
- 1 tablespoon cornstarch
- 4 tablespoons Kikkoman Soy Sauce, divided
- 1/2 teaspoon sugar
- 1 clove garlic, minced
- 1 1/4 cups water
- 4 teaspoons cornstarch
- 1 1/2 teaspoons distilled white vinegar
- 1/8 to 1/4 teaspoon ground red pepper (cayenne)
- 3 tablespoons vegetable oil, divided
- 3 cups bite-size cauliflowerets
  Salt
- 1 onion, chunked and separated
- 1 green pepper, chunked

Cut beef across grain into thin strips. Combine 1 tablespoon *each* cornstarch and soy sauce with sugar and garlic in small bowl; stir in beef. Let stand 15 minutes. Meanwhile, combine water, remaining 3 tablespoons soy sauce, 4 teaspoons cornstarch, vinegar and red pepper; set aside. Heat 1 tablespoon oil in hot wok or large skillet over high heat. Add beef and stir-fry 1 minute; remove. Heat remaining 2 tablespoons oil in same pan. Add cauliflowerets; lightly sprinkle with salt and stir-fry 2 minutes. Add onion and green pepper; stir-fry 4 minutes. Stir in beef and soy sauce mixture; cook and stir until sauce boils and thickens.

GINGER BEEF WITH BOK CHOY

Makes 4 servings

¾ pound boneless tender beef steak
    (sirloin, rib eye or top loin)
3 tablespoons Kikkoman Lite Soy Sauce,
    divided
1 tablespoon cornstarch
1 tablespoon dry sherry
1 teaspoon minced fresh ginger root
1 clove garlic, minced
¾ cup water
2 teaspoons cornstarch
½ pound bok choy cabbage or romaine
    lettuce
2 tablespoons vegetable oil, divided
1 medium onion, cut into ½-inch strips
1 tablespoon slivered fresh ginger root

Cut beef across grain into thin slices. Combine 1 tablespoon *each* lite soy sauce, cornstarch and sherry with minced ginger and garlic in medium bowl; stir in beef. Let stand 30 minutes. Meanwhile, combine water, 2 teaspoons cornstarch and remaining 2 tablespoons lite soy sauce; set aside. Separate and rinse bok choy; pat dry. Cut leaves crosswise into 1-inch strips, separating stems from leaves. Heat 1 tablespoon oil in hot wok or large skillet over high heat. Add beef and stir-fry 1 minute; remove. Heat remaining 1 tablespoon oil in same pan. Add onion and slivered ginger; stir-fry 2 minutes. Add bok choy stems; stir-fry 1 minute. Add leaves; stir-fry 1 minute longer. Add beef and soy sauce mixture; cook and stir until sauce boils and thickens. Serve immediately.

Ginger Beef with Bok Choy

Beef with Leafy Greens

BEEF WITH LEAFY GREENS

Makes 2 to 3 servings

3/4 pound romaine lettuce

1/2 pound boneless tender beef steak
   (sirloin, rib eye or top loin)

4 tablespoons Kikkoman Stir-Fry Sauce,
   divided

1 clove garlic, minced

2 tablespoons vegetable oil, divided

1 medium onion, chunked

1 teaspoon minced fresh ginger root

8 cherry tomatoes, halved *or* 1 medium
   tomato, chunked

2 tablespoons chopped unsalted peanuts

Separate and rinse lettuce; pat dry. Cut leaves crosswise into 1-inch strips; set aside. Cut beef across grain into thin slices. Combine 1 tablespoon stir-fry sauce and garlic in small bowl; stir in beef to coat. Heat 1 tablespoon oil in hot wok or large skillet over high heat. Add beef and stir-fry 1 minute; remove. Heat remaining 1 tablespoon oil in same pan. Add onion and ginger; stir-fry 2 minutes. Add lettuce; stir-fry 2 minutes longer. Add beef, tomatoes and remaining 3 tablespoons stir-fry sauce; cook and stir until vegetables are coated with sauce and tomatoes are just heated through. Serve immediately with peanuts.

SICHUAN BEEF STIR-FRY

Makes 4 servings

1 pound boneless tender beef steak
  (sirloin, rib eye or top loin)
2 tablespoons cornstarch
3 tablespoons Kikkoman Soy Sauce,
  divided
½ teaspoon sugar
½ teaspoon crushed red pepper
1 large clove garlic, minced
⅔ cup water
1½ teaspoons cornstarch
3 tablespoons vegetable oil, divided
¼ pound green onions and tops, cut into
  1½-inch lengths, separating whites
  from tops

Cut beef across grain into thin slices, then into strips. Combine 2 tablespoons *each* cornstarch and soy sauce with sugar, red pepper and garlic in medium bowl; stir in beef. Let stand 20 minutes. Meanwhile, combine water, remaining 1 tablespoon soy sauce and 1½ teaspoons cornstarch; set aside. Heat 2 tablespoons oil in hot wok or large skillet over high heat. Add beef and stir-fry 1 minute; remove. Heat remaining 1 tablespoon oil in same pan; add white parts of green onions and stir-fry 1 minute. Stir in beef, soy sauce mixture and green onion tops. Cook and stir until mixture boils and thickens. Serve immediately.

BEEF WITH SNOW PEAS & CAULIFLOWER

Makes 2 to 3 servings

½ pound boneless tender beef steak
  (sirloin, rib eye or top loin)
2 tablespoons cornstarch, divided
3 tablespoons Kikkoman Soy Sauce,
  divided
½ teaspoon sugar
1 clove garlic, minced
1 cup water, divided
¼ to ½ teaspoon crushed red pepper
3 tablespoons vegetable oil, divided
½ pound fresh snow peas, trimmed
1 small head cauliflower, separated into
  flowerets
2 medium tomatoes, chunked
  Hot cooked rice

Cut beef across grain into thin slices. Combine 1 tablespoon *each* cornstarch and soy sauce with sugar and garlic in small bowl; stir in beef. Let stand 15 minutes. Meanwhile, combine ½ cup water, remaining 1 tablespoon cornstarch and 2 tablespoons soy sauce with red pepper; set aside. Heat 1 tablespoon oil in hot wok or large skillet over high heat. Add beef and stir-fry 1 minute; remove. Heat 1 tablespoon oil in same pan. Add snow peas and stir-fry 2 minutes; remove. Heat remaining 1 tablespoon oil in same pan; add cauliflowerets and stir-fry 2 minutes. Add remaining ½ cup water; cover and steam 3 minutes. Stir in beef, snow peas, tomatoes and soy sauce mixture. Cook and stir until mixture boils and thickens. Serve immediately with rice.

KOREAN RIBS

Makes 4 servings

4 pounds beef short ribs, 2½ inches
  long
⅔ cup Kikkoman Teriyaki Sauce
1 tablespoon sesame seed, toasted
1 teaspoon sugar
2 teaspoons Tabasco pepper sauce
2 large cloves garlic, pressed

Score meaty side of ribs, opposite bone, ½ inch apart, ½ inch deep, lengthwise and crosswise. Place ribs in large plastic bag. Combine teriyaki sauce, sesame seed, sugar, pepper sauce and garlic; pour over ribs. Press air out of bag; tie top securely. Refrigerate 4 hours, turning bag over occasionally. Remove ribs and broil or grill 4 inches from heat source or hot coals 15 to 18 minutes, or until outsides of ribs are brown and crisp. Turn ribs over occasionally during cooking.

BEEF & TOMATO STIR-FRY SALAD

Makes 4 to 6 servings

- 1 pound boneless tender beef steak (sirloin, rib eye or top loin)
- 1 tablespoon cornstarch
- 4 tablespoons Kikkoman Soy Sauce, divided
- 1/2 teaspoon sugar
- 1 clove garlic, pressed
- 2 tablespoons water
- 1 tablespoon red wine vinegar
- 1 tablespoon tomato catsup
- 3 tablespoons vegetable oil, divided
- 1 teaspoon onion powder
- 4 cups shredded iceberg lettuce
- 2 stalks celery, cut diagonally into thin slices
- 1 green pepper, cut into julienne strips
- 2 teaspoons minced fresh ginger root
- 15 cherry tomatoes, halved

Cut beef across grain into thin strips. Combine cornstarch, 2 tablespoons soy sauce, sugar and garlic in medium bowl; stir in beef. Let stand 15 minutes. Meanwhile, combine remaining 2 tablespoons soy sauce, water, vinegar, catsup, 1 tablespoon oil and onion powder; set aside. Line large shallow bowl or large platter with lettuce. Heat 1 tablespoon oil in hot wok or large skillet over high heat. Add beef and stir-fry 1 minute; remove. Heat remaining 1 tablespoon oil in same pan. Add celery, green pepper and ginger; stir-fry 1 minute. Remove pan from heat; stir in tomatoes, beef and soy sauce mixture. Spoon mixture over lettuce; toss well to combine before serving. Serve immediately.

Beef & Tomato Stir-Fry Salad

KOREAN BEEF & VEGETABLE SALAD

Makes 4 servings

3/4 pound boneless beef sirloin steak
1 tablespoon cornstarch
2 tablespoons Kikkoman Lite Soy Sauce
2 cloves garlic, minced
1 teaspoon sesame seed, toasted
1/4 teaspoon crushed red pepper
 Korean Dressing (recipe follows)
3/4 pound bok choy cabbage
 Boiling water
1/4 pound fresh snow peas, trimmed
1 small cucumber
1/4 pound fresh bean sprouts
1 carrot, cut into julienne strips
1 tablespoon vegetable oil

Cut beef across grain into thin slices, then into strips. Combine cornstarch, lite soy sauce, garlic, sesame seed and pepper in small bowl; stir in beef. Let stand 15 minutes. Meanwhile, prepare Korean Dressing. Separate and rinse bok choy; pat dry. Slice bok choy stems and leaves crosswise into thin strips. Pour boiling water over snow peas in bowl; let stand 30 seconds. Drain; cool under cold water and drain thoroughly. Cut cucumber in half lengthwise; remove seeds. Cut halves crosswise into thin slices. Arrange vegetables on large platter or in shallow bowl; cover and refrigerate until chilled. Heat oil in hot wok or large skillet over high heat. Add beef; stir-fry 2 minutes. Remove from heat and cool slightly; spoon onto platter with vegetables. To serve, pour desired amount of Korean Dressing over meat and vegetables; toss to combine. Garnish as desired.

KOREAN DRESSING:

Whisk together *2/3 cup mayonnaise, 4 teaspoons lemon juice, 1 tablespoon Kikkoman Lite Soy Sauce, 1 tablespoon minced green onion, 1 tablespoon water* and *2 teaspoons sesame seed, toasted.* Cover and refrigerate until ready to serve.

BROCCOLI & BEEF STIR-FRY

Makes 2 to 3 servings

1/2 pound boneless tender beef steak
 (sirloin, rib eye or top loin)
1 tablespoon cornstarch
4 tablespoons Kikkoman Soy Sauce,
 divided
1 teaspoon sugar
1 teaspoon minced fresh ginger root
1 clove garlic, minced
1 pound fresh broccoli
1 1/4 cups water
4 teaspoons cornstarch
3 tablespoons vegetable oil, divided
1 onion, chunked
 Hot cooked rice

Cut beef across grain into thin slices. Combine 1 tablespoon *each* cornstarch and soy sauce with sugar, ginger and garlic in small bowl; stir in beef. Let stand 15 minutes. Meanwhile, remove flowerets from broccoli; cut in half lengthwise. Peel stalks; cut crosswise into 1/8-inch slices. Combine water, 4 teaspoons cornstarch and remaining 3 tablespoons soy sauce; set aside. Heat 1 tablespoon oil in hot wok or large skillet over high heat. Add beef and stir-fry 1 minute; remove. Heat remaining 2 tablespoons oil in same pan. Add broccoli and onion; stir-fry 4 minutes. Stir in beef and soy sauce mixture. Cook and stir until mixture boils and thickens. Serve immediately over rice.

Korean Beef & Vegetable Salad

Simply Super Sukiyaki

SIMPLY SUPER SUKIYAKI

Makes 4 to 6 servings

1 block tofu
1/2 cup Kikkoman Soy Sauce
1/2 cup water
2 tablespoons sugar
3/4 pound ground beef
1 medium-size yellow onion, thinly sliced
1 pound fresh spinach, trimmed, washed and drained
1 bunch green onions and tops, cut into 2-inch lengths, separating whites from tops
1/4 pound fresh mushrooms, sliced

Cut tofu into 1-inch cubes; drain well on several layers of paper towels. Meanwhile, combine soy sauce, water and sugar; set aside. Brown beef in Dutch oven or large skillet over medium heat, stirring to break beef into large chunks. Add yellow onion; cook 1 minute. Add spinach, white parts of green onions, mushrooms and soy sauce mixture; cook until spinach wilts, stirring constantly. Gently stir in tofu and green onion tops. Cook 5 to 7 minutes, or until vegetables are tender and tofu is seasoned with sauce.

STUFFED TERIYAKI STEAKS

Makes 6 to 8 servings

2 boneless beef sirloin steaks, each cut 1/2 inch thick (about 1 pound each)
1/2 cup Kikkoman Teriyaki Sauce
6 green onions and tops
Boiling water

Pound each steak evenly to 1/4-inch thickness. Spread steaks out in large pan; pour in teriyaki sauce and turn steaks over to thoroughly coat each piece. Marinate 15 minutes, turning steaks over occasionally. Meanwhile, place green onions in shallow pan. Pour enough boiling water over onions to cover; drain immediately and cool. Remove steaks from marinade; spread out flat. Place 3 green onions lengthwise in center of each steak. Roll steaks up lengthwise, jelly-roll fashion, around onions; secure with string or wooden picks. Broil or grill 4 to 6 inches from heat source or hot coals 10 to 12 minutes (for rare), or to desired doneness, turning rolls over frequently. To serve, cut rolls crosswise into 3-inch pieces; remove string or picks.

RED-COOKED SHORT RIBS

Makes 4 servings

- 3 pounds beef short ribs
- $\frac{1}{3}$ to $\frac{1}{2}$ cup all-purpose flour
- 2 tablespoons vegetable oil
- $1\frac{3}{4}$ cups water, divided
- $\frac{1}{2}$ cup Kikkoman Teriyaki Sauce
- 1 clove garlic, pressed
- $\frac{1}{2}$ teaspoon ground ginger
- $\frac{1}{8}$ teaspoon ground cloves

Coat ribs thoroughly with flour; reserve $\frac{1}{4}$ cup excess flour. Heat oil in Dutch oven or large saucepan over medium heat. Add ribs and brown slowly on all sides; drain off excess oil. Combine $1\frac{1}{4}$ cups water, teriyaki sauce, garlic, ginger and cloves; pour over ribs. Cover; simmer 2 hours, or until ribs are tender. Meanwhile, blend reserved flour and remaining $\frac{1}{2}$ cup water. Remove ribs to serving platter; keep warm. Pour pan drippings into large measuring cup; skim off fat. Add enough water to measure $2\frac{1}{2}$ cups; return to pan and bring to boil. Gradually stir in flour mixture. Cook and stir until thickened; serve with ribs.

CANTONESE STIR-FRY

Makes 4 servings

- $\frac{3}{4}$ pound boneless beef sirloin, lean pork or chicken
- 1 tablespoon Kikkoman Stir-Fry Sauce
- 2 tablespoons vegetable oil, divided
- 2 small zucchini, cut crosswise into $\frac{1}{4}$-inch-thick slices
- 1 onion, chunked
- 12 cherry tomatoes, halved
- $\frac{1}{4}$ cup Kikkoman Stir-Fry Sauce

Cut beef, pork or chicken across grain into thin slices, then into slivers; coat with 1 tablespoon stir-fry sauce. Heat 1 tablespoon oil in hot wok or large skillet over high heat. Add beef and stir-fry 1 minute (stir-fry pork or chicken 2 minutes); remove. Heat remaining 1 tablespoon oil in same pan. Add zucchini and onion; stir-fry 4 minutes. Stir in beef, tomatoes and $\frac{1}{4}$ cup stir-fry sauce. Cook and stir until beef and vegetables are coated with sauce and tomatoes are heated through. Serve immediately.

Red-Cooked Short Ribs

MONGOLIAN BEEF

Makes 4 servings

3/4 pound boneless tender beef steak
    (sirloin, rib eye or top loin)
3 tablespoons cornstarch, divided
4 tablespoons Kikkoman Teriyaki Sauce,
    divided
1 tablespoon dry sherry
1 clove garlic, minced
1 cup water
1 teaspoon distilled white vinegar
1/4 to 1/2 teaspoon crushed red pepper
2 tablespoons vegetable oil, divided
2 carrots, cut diagonally into thin slices
1 onion, chunked and separated
1 green pepper, chunked

Cut beef across grain into strips, then into 1½-inch squares. Combine 2 tablespoons cornstarch, 1 tablespoon teriyaki sauce, sherry and garlic in medium bowl; stir in beef. Let stand 30 minutes. Meanwhile, combine water, remaining 1 tablespoon cornstarch, 3 tablespoons teriyaki sauce, vinegar and red pepper; set aside. Heat 1 tablespoon oil in hot wok or large skillet over high heat. Add beef and stir-fry 1 minute; remove. Heat remaining 1 tablespoon oil in same pan. Add carrots, onion and green pepper; stir-fry 4 minutes. Add beef and teriyaki sauce mixture; cook and stir until sauce boils and thickens.

Mongolian Beef

Thai Beef Salad

THAI BEEF SALAD

Makes 4 servings

1 boneless beef sirloin steak, about
   3/4 inch thick (about 1 pound)
3 tablespoons Kikkoman Lite Soy Sauce
3 tablespoons lime juice
2 teaspoons brown sugar
2 large cloves garlic, pressed
2 tablespoons vegetable oil
2 heads butter lettuce, washed and
   drained
2 tablespoons chopped fresh mint
2 tablespoons chopped fresh cilantro
2 tablespoons chopped unsalted roasted
   peanuts

Place steak in large plastic bag. Blend lite soy sauce, lime juice, brown sugar and garlic, stirring until sugar dissolves. Remove 1/4 cup mixture; pour over steak. Press air out of bag; tie top securely. Turn over several times to coat both sides. Marinate 30 minutes, turning bag over occasionally. Meanwhile, combine remaining soy sauce mixture and oil in jar with screw-top lid. Tear lettuce into bite-size pieces and toss with mint and cilantro in large bowl; cover and refrigerate until chilled. Remove steak from marinade and place on rack of broiler pan. Broil 4 minutes on each side (for rare), or to desired degree of doneness. Cut steak across grain into thin slices. Shake dressing and pour over greens; toss to combine. Turn out onto large serving platter; arrange beef slices over greens. Sprinkle peanuts over greens and beef. Serve immediately.

PORK

ORIENTAL PORK BUNDLES

Makes 4 to 6 servings

    Plum Sauce (recipe follows)
 1/3 cup Kikkoman Stir-Fry Sauce
   1 clove garlic, pressed
 1/2 pound boneless lean pork, diced
 1/2 teaspoon vegetable oil
   2 eggs, beaten
   2 tablespoons vegetable oil, divided
   2 stalks celery, diced
   1 medium carrot, diced
   1 small onion, diced
   2 ounces fresh mushrooms, coarsely chopped
   6 (8-inch) flour tortillas, warmed
   3 cups finely shredded iceberg lettuce

Prepare Plum Sauce; cool while preparing filling. Combine stir-fry sauce and garlic. Coat pork with 1 tablespoon stir-fry sauce mixture; let stand 10 minutes. Meanwhile, heat 1/2 teaspoon oil in hot wok or large skillet over medium-high heat. Pour in eggs and scramble; remove. Heat 1 tablespoon oil in same pan. Add pork and stir-fry 3 minutes; remove. Heat remaining 1 tablespoon oil in same pan. Add celery, carrot, onion and mushrooms; stir-fry 4 minutes. Stir in eggs, pork and remaining stir-fry sauce mixture. Cook and stir just until pork and vegetables are coated with sauce. Spread 1 tablespoon Plum Sauce on each tortilla; top with desired amount of shredded lettuce and pork mixture. Wrap or fold over to enclose filling.

PLUM SAUCE:

Combine *1/4 cup plum jam, 2 tablespoons Kikkoman Stir-Fry Sauce* and *1/2 teaspoon distilled white vinegar* in small saucepan. Cook, stirring constantly, over medium-high heat until mixture comes to a boil and is smooth.

PINEAPPLE-GLAZED SPARERIBS

Makes 4 servings

3 to 4 pounds pork spareribs
1 can (20 oz.) sliced pineapple in syrup
1/2 cup Kikkoman Soy Sauce
1/4 cup tomato catsup
2 tablespoons brown sugar, packed
1 clove garlic, pressed

Cut ribs into serving pieces; place, meaty side down, in shallow foil-lined baking pan. Bake in 450°F. oven 20 minutes. Meanwhile, drain pineapple; reserve syrup. Combine syrup, soy sauce, catsup, brown sugar and garlic. Remove ribs from oven and drain off drippings. *Reduce oven temperature to 325°F.* Pour soy sauce mixture evenly over ribs; cover pan loosely with foil. Continue baking 45 minutes. Turn ribs over and top with pineapple slices. Brush ribs and pineapple thoroughly with sauce in pan. Return to oven and bake, uncovered, 15 minutes, or until pineapple is heated through. Brush ribs with pan drippings before serving.

CASHEW PORK STIR-FRY

Makes 4 servings

3/4 pound boneless lean pork
1 tablespoon Kikkoman Stir-Fry Sauce
3 tablespoons vegetable oil, divided
2 stalks celery, cut diagonally into 1/2-inch slices
1 onion, chunked
1 large green pepper, chunked
1/4 pound fresh mushrooms, sliced
2 medium tomatoes, chunked
1/4 cup Kikkoman Stir-Fry Sauce
1/4 cup roasted cashews

Cut pork across grain into thin slices; coat with 1 tablespoon stir-fry sauce. Heat 1 tablespoon oil in hot wok or large skillet over medium-high heat. Add pork and stir-fry 3 minutes; remove. Wipe out pan with paper towel. Heat remaining 2 tablespoons oil in same pan over high heat. Add celery, onion and green pepper; stir-fry 2 minutes. Add mushrooms and stir-fry 2 minutes longer. Add pork, tomatoes and 1/4 cup stir-fry sauce. Cook and stir only until tomatoes are heated through. Just before serving, sprinkle cashews over pork and vegetables.

HAWAIIAN ROAST PORK

Makes 6 servings

1 (3-pound) boneless pork shoulder roast (Boston butt)
1/2 cup Kikkoman Soy Sauce
1 1/2 teaspoons liquid smoke seasoning

Cut pork in half lengthwise. Place halves in large plastic bag. Combine soy sauce and liquid smoke; pour over pork. Press air out of bag; tie top securely. Turn over several times to coat pieces well. Refrigerate 8 hours or overnight, turning bag over occasionally. Remove pork from marinade and place in shallow baking pan; cover with aluminum foil. Bake at 350°F. 30 minutes. Discard foil; turn pieces over. Bake 1 hour longer, or until meat thermometer inserted into thickest part registers 170°F. To serve, cut across grain into thin slices.

HUNAN PORK STIR-FRY

Makes 2 to 3 servings

½ pound boneless lean pork
2 teaspoons cornstarch
6 teaspoons Kikkoman Lite Soy Sauce, divided
2 cloves garlic, minced and divided
¾ cup water
1 tablespoon cornstarch
⅛ to ¼ teaspoon crushed red pepper
3 tablespoons vegetable oil, divided
3 cups bite-size cauliflowerets
1 medium-size green pepper, chunked
2 medium tomatoes, cut into eighths
  Hot cooked rice

Cut pork across grain into thin slices, then into strips. Combine 2 teaspoons *each* cornstarch and lite soy sauce with ½ of the garlic in small bowl; stir in pork. Let stand 30 minutes. Meanwhile, combine water, 1 tablespoon cornstarch, remaining 4 teaspoons lite soy sauce and red pepper; set aside. Heat 1 tablespoon oil in hot wok or large skillet over high heat. Add pork and stir-fry 2 minutes; remove. Heat remaining 2 tablespoons oil in same pan over medium-high heat. Add cauliflowerets and remaining garlic; stir-fry 2 minutes. Add green pepper; stir-fry 3 minutes. Stir in tomatoes, pork and soy sauce mixture. Cook and stir gently until sauce boils and thickens. Serve with rice.

Hunan Pork Stir-Fry

Tofu & Vegetable Stir-Fry

TOFU & VEGETABLE STIR-FRY

Makes 4 servings

¹/₂ block tofu

1 pound napa (Chinese cabbage) or romaine lettuce*

¹/₂ cup water

2 tablespoons cornstarch, divided

4 tablespoons Kikkoman Soy Sauce, divided

¹/₄ pound boneless lean pork

2 teaspoons minced fresh ginger root

1 clove garlic, minced

¹/₂ teaspoon sugar

2 tablespoons vegetable oil, divided

1 medium onion, chunked

2 medium tomatoes, chunked

Cut tofu into ¹/₂-inch cubes; drain well on several layers of paper towels. Separate and rinse cabbage; pat dry. Cut leaves crosswise into 1-inch strips; set aside. Blend water, 1 tablespoon cornstarch and 3 tablespoons soy sauce; set aside. Cut pork into thin slices, then into thin strips. Combine remaining 1 tablespoon cornstarch and 1 tablespoon soy sauce, ginger, garlic and sugar in small bowl; stir in pork. Heat 1 tablespoon oil in hot wok or large skillet over high heat. Add pork and stir-fry 2 minutes; remove. Heat remaining 1 tablespoon oil in same pan. Add onion; stir-fry 2 minutes. Add cabbage; stir-fry 1 minute. Add tomatoes, pork and soy sauce mixture. Cook and stir gently until sauce boils and thickens. Gently fold in tofu; heat through.

*If using romaine, increase water to ²/₃ cup.

CELEBRATION PORK & RICE

Makes 4 servings

- ³/₄ pound boneless lean pork
- 6 tablespoons Kikkoman Stir-Fry Sauce, divided
- ¹/₈ to ¹/₄ teaspoon pepper
- 2 tablespoons vegetable oil, divided
- 1¹/₂ cups frozen peas & carrots, thawed
- ¹/₂ cup chopped onion
- ¹/₈ teaspoon salt
- 3¹/₂ cups cold cooked rice

Cut pork across grain into thin slices, then into slivers; combine with 2 tablespoons stir-fry sauce. Stir pepper into remaining 4 tablespoons stir-fry sauce; set aside. Heat 1 tablespoon oil in hot wok or large skillet over high heat. Add pork and stir-fry 3 minutes; remove. Heat remaining 1 tablespoon oil in same pan. Add peas & carrots, onion and salt; stir-fry 2 minutes. Remove from heat and gently stir in rice to combine. Return to medium-high heat; stir in pork and stir-fry sauce mixture. Cook and stir until rice is thoroughly heated and coated with sauce.

BAKE & GLAZE TERI RIBS

Makes 4 servings

- 3 pounds pork spareribs
- ¹/₂ teaspoon garlic powder
- ¹/₂ teaspoon pepper
- ²/₃ cup Kikkoman Teriyaki Baste & Glaze
- ¹/₂ teaspoon grated lemon peel

Cut ribs into serving pieces; place, meaty side up, in shallow foil-lined baking pan. Sprinkle garlic powder and pepper evenly over ribs; cover pan loosely with foil. Bake in 350°F. oven 45 minutes. Meanwhile, combine teriyaki baste & glaze and lemon peel. Remove foil and brush both sides of ribs with baste & glaze mixture. Cover and bake 40 minutes longer, or until ribs are tender, brushing with baste & glaze mixture occasionally.

Celebration Pork & Rice

PORK CHOPS TERIYAKI

Makes 4 to 6 servings

1 can (8 oz.) pineapple chunks in juice
1 tablespoon vegetable oil
6 boneless pork chops, ¾ inch thick
½ cup Kikkoman Teriyaki Sauce
¼ cup water
1 clove garlic, minced
1 tablespoon sesame seed, toasted
2 teaspoons grated fresh ginger root
1 tablespoon cornstarch
1 tablespoon water
½ cup finely chopped green onions and
tops

Drain pineapple; reserve juice. Heat oil in Dutch oven over medium-high heat. Brown pork chops on both sides in hot oil. Combine reserved juice, teriyaki sauce, ¼ cup water, garlic, sesame seed and ginger; pour over chops and simmer, covered, 30 minutes. Turn chops over and continue cooking, covered, 30 minutes longer, or until chops are tender; remove. Dissolve cornstarch in 1 tablespoon water and stir into pan juices. Cook and stir until sauce boils and thickens. Stir in pineapple chunks and green onions, cooking until pineapple is heated through. Return chops to pan and coat both sides with sauce.

SICHUAN PORK SALAD

Makes 2 to 3 servings

½ pound boneless lean pork
4 tablespoons Kikkoman Teriyaki Sauce,
divided
⅛ to ¼ teaspoon crushed red pepper
1 cup water
2 tablespoons cornstarch
1 tablespoon distilled white vinegar
2 tablespoons vegetable oil, divided
1 onion, chunked and separated
12 radishes, thinly sliced
2 medium zucchini, cut into julienne
strips
Salt
4 cups shredded lettuce

Cut pork across grain into thin slices, then into narrow strips. Combine pork, 1 tablespoon teriyaki sauce and red pepper in small bowl; set aside. Combine water, cornstarch, remaining 3 tablespoons teriyaki sauce and vinegar; set aside. Heat 1 tablespoon oil in hot wok or large skillet over high heat. Add pork and stir-fry 2 minutes; remove. Heat remaining 1 tablespoon oil in same pan. Add onion; stir-fry 2 minutes. Add radishes and zucchini; lightly sprinkle with salt and stir-fry 1 minute longer. Stir in pork and teriyaki sauce mixture. Cook and stir until mixture boils and thickens. Spoon over bed of lettuce on serving platter; serve immediately.

SPICY SICHUAN PORK STEW

Makes 6 servings

2 pounds boneless pork shoulder (Boston
butt)
¼ cup all-purpose flour
2 tablespoons vegetable oil
1¾ cups water, divided
¼ cup Kikkoman Soy Sauce
3 tablespoons dry sherry
2 cloves garlic, pressed
1 teaspoon minced fresh ginger root
½ teaspoon crushed red pepper
¼ teaspoon fennel seed, crushed
8 green onions and tops, cut into 1-inch
lengths, separating whites from tops
2 large carrots, chunked
Hot cooked rice

Cut pork into 1-inch cubes. Coat in flour; reserve 2 tablespoons flour. Heat oil in Dutch oven or large pan over medium-high heat; brown pork on all sides in hot oil. Add 1½ cups water, soy sauce, sherry, garlic, ginger, red pepper, fennel and white parts of green onions. Cover pan; bring to boil. Reduce heat and simmer 30 minutes. Add carrots; simmer, covered, 30 minutes longer, or until pork and carrots are tender. Meanwhile, combine reserved flour and remaining ¼ cup water; set aside. Stir green onion tops into pork mixture; simmer 1 minute. Add flour mixture; bring to boil. Cook and stir until mixture is slightly thickened. Serve over rice.

Spicy Sichuan Pork Stew

CHINESE TEA-SMOKED RIBS

Makes 3 to 4 servings

16 bags or 6 tablespoons loose black tea
  leaves
1½ teaspoons fennel seed, crushed
 ½ teaspoon ground ginger
 ½ teaspoon ground cloves
 ½ teaspoon black pepper
   Nonstick cooking spray
  3 pounds pork spareribs, sawed into
    thirds across bones
 ½ cup Kikkoman Teriyaki Baste & Glaze
  1 tablespoon tomato catsup
  1 clove garlic, minced
 ⅛ teaspoon ground red pepper (cayenne)

Remove tea leaves from bags; combine with fennel, ginger, cloves and black pepper. Thoroughly spray large rack and large shallow baking pan with cooking spray. Sprinkle tea mixture evenly in pan. Cut ribs into 1-rib pieces and place, meaty side up, on rack over tea mixture. Cover pan with foil and bake at 350°F. 30 minutes. Meanwhile, combine teriyaki baste & glaze, catsup, garlic and red pepper; set aside. Remove ribs from oven; *reduce oven temperature to 325°F.* Reserving about 2 tablespoonfuls, brush both sides of ribs with baste & glaze mixture; return to oven and bake, uncovered, 40 minutes. Brush tops of ribs with reserved baste & glaze mixture; bake 5 minutes longer. Garnish as desired.

Chinese Tea-Smoked Ribs

Colorful Stir-Fried Pork

KUNG PAO PORK

Makes 4 servings

3/4 pound boneless lean pork
4 tablespoons Kikkoman Soy Sauce, divided
1/4 cup water
2 tablespoons sugar
2 tablespoons lemon juice
2 teaspoons cornstarch
1/4 teaspoon crushed red pepper
2 tablespoons vegetable oil
2 cloves garlic, minced
1 small red bell pepper, chunked
1 small onion, chunked
1/4 cup unsalted roasted peanuts

Cut pork into 1/2-inch cubes; combine with 2 tablespoons soy sauce. Let stand 30 minutes. Meanwhile, combine water, remaining 2 tablespoons soy sauce, sugar, lemon juice, cornstarch and crushed red pepper; set aside. Heat oil in hot wok or large skillet over high heat. Add pork and garlic; stir-fry 3 minutes. Add red bell pepper and onion; stir-fry 3 minutes. Add soy sauce mixture; cook and stir until sauce boils and thickens. Remove from heat and stir in peanuts. Serve immediately.

COLORFUL STIR-FRIED PORK

Makes 4 servings

1/3 cup Kikkoman Stir-Fry Sauce
1 teaspoon distilled white vinegar
1/4 to 1/2 teaspoon crushed red pepper
3/4 pound boneless lean pork
1 tablespoon Kikkoman Stir-Fry Sauce
3 tablespoons vegetable oil, divided
2 medium carrots, cut into julienne strips
1 medium onion, halved and sliced
1/4 pound fresh snow peas, trimmed and cut lengthwise in half

Combine 1/3 cup stir-fry sauce, vinegar and red pepper; set aside. Cut pork across grain into thin slices, then into strips; coat with 1 tablespoon stir-fry sauce. Heat 1 tablespoon oil in hot wok or large skillet over high heat. Add pork and stir-fry 2 minutes; remove. Heat remaining 2 tablespoons oil in same pan. Add carrots, onion and snow peas; stir-fry 4 minutes. Stir in pork and stir-fry sauce mixture. Cook and stir just until pork and vegetables are coated with sauce. Serve immediately.

Snake Alley Noodles

SNAKE ALLEY NOODLES

Makes 4 to 6 servings

- 3/4 pound uncooked spaghetti
- 1 cup water
- 1/4 cup Kikkoman Soy Sauce
- 2 tablespoons dry sherry
- 4 teaspoons cornstarch
- 1 pound ground pork
- 1 tablespoon minced fresh ginger root
- 2 cloves garlic, minced
- 1/2 teaspoon crushed red pepper
- 3/4 cup chopped green onions and tops
- 1/2 pound cooked baby shrimp

Cook spaghetti according to package directions, omitting salt; drain and keep warm on serving plate. Meanwhile, combine water, soy sauce, sherry and cornstarch; set aside. Heat wok or large skillet over medium heat. Add pork, ginger, garlic and red pepper; stir-fry until pork is cooked. Add green onions; stir-fry 1 minute. Add soy sauce mixture. Cook and stir until mixture boils and thickens slightly. Stir in shrimp; heat through. Pour over spaghetti; toss to combine before serving.

CHINESE BARBECUED PORK

Makes 6 servings

- 1 (3-pound) boneless pork shoulder roast (Boston butt)
- 1/2 cup Kikkoman Soy Sauce
- 2 tablespoons dry sherry
- 2 tablespoons honey
- 1 teaspoon minced fresh ginger root
- 1 clove garlic, pressed
- 1/4 teaspoon red food coloring (optional)

Cut pork in half lengthwise. Pierce all sides of both halves with fork; place halves in large plastic bag. Combine soy sauce, sherry, honey, ginger, garlic and food coloring; pour over pork. Press air out of bag; tie top securely. Turn over several times to coat pieces well. Refrigerate 8 hours or overnight, turning bag over occasionally. Reserving marinade, remove pork and place on rack in shallow baking pan; cover loosely with aluminum foil. Bake at 325°F. 30 minutes. Discard foil; continue baking 1 hour and 15 minutes longer, or until meat thermometer inserted into thickest part registers 170°F. Brush pieces with reserved marinade 2 or 3 times during baking. To serve, cut across grain into thin slices. Garnish as desired.

PORK AND PEANUT STIR-FRY

Makes 2 to 3 servings

- ¼ pound boneless lean pork
- 4 teaspoons cornstarch, divided
- 3 tablespoons Kikkoman Lite Soy Sauce, divided
- 1 teaspoon minced fresh ginger root
- ½ cup water
- 2 teaspoons distilled white vinegar
- ¼ teaspoon garlic powder
- 2 tablespoons vegetable oil, divided
- 1 medium onion, sliced
- 1 medium carrot, cut diagonally into ⅛-inch-thick slices
- 2 medium zucchini, cut diagonally into ⅛-inch-thick slices
- ⅓ cup unsalted roasted peanuts
  Hot cooked rice (optional)

Cut pork across grain into thin slices, then into strips. Combine 2 teaspoons *each* cornstarch and lite soy sauce with ginger in small bowl; stir in pork. Let stand 15 minutes. Meanwhile, combine water, remaining 2 teaspoons cornstarch, 2 tablespoons plus 1 teaspoon lite soy sauce, vinegar and garlic powder; set aside. Heat 1 tablespoon oil in hot wok or large skillet over high heat. Add pork and stir-fry 2 minutes; remove. Heat remaining 1 tablespoon oil in same pan. Add onion and carrot; stir-fry 2 minutes. Add zucchini; stir-fry 2 minutes. Stir in pork and soy sauce mixture. Cook and stir until mixture boils and thickens. Stir in peanuts; serve immediately with rice.

Pork and Peanut Stir-Fry

CRISPY LITE SPARERIBS

Makes 4 to 6 servings

4 pounds pork spareribs, sawed into thirds across bones
1/4 cup Kikkoman Lite Soy Sauce
2 tablespoons dry sherry
1 clove garlic, pressed
Mandarin Peach Sauce (recipe follows)

Cut ribs into 1-rib pieces. Place in steamer basket or on steamer rack. Set basket in large pot or wok of boiling water. (Do not allow water level to reach ribs.) Cover and steam 30 minutes. Meanwhile, combine lite soy sauce, sherry and garlic in large bowl; add ribs and stir to coat each piece well. Marinate 1 hour, stirring frequently. Remove ribs and place, meaty side up, on rack of broiler pan. Bake in 425°F. oven 15 minutes, or until crispy. Serve with warm Mandarin Peach Sauce.

MANDARIN PEACH SAUCE:

Drain *1 can (16 oz.) cling peach slices in juice or extra light syrup; reserve liquid for another use. Place peaches in blender container. Process on high speed until smooth; pour into small saucepan. Combine 3 tablespoons Kikkoman Teriyaki Sauce and 1 tablespoon cornstarch; stir into peaches with 1 tablespoon sugar, 1/4 teaspoon fennel seed, crushed, 1/4 teaspoon pepper and 1/8 teaspoon ground cloves. Bring mixture to boil over medium heat. Simmer until sauce thickens, about 2 minutes, stirring constantly. Remove from heat and stir in 1/8 teaspoon garlic powder. Makes 1 cup.*

HAWAIIAN PORK STEW

Makes 6 servings

2 pounds boneless pork shoulder (Boston butt)
1/4 cup all-purpose flour
1 teaspoon ground ginger
2 tablespoons vegetable oil
1 can (8 oz.) pineapple chunks in juice
1 3/4 cups water, divided
1/3 cup Kikkoman Teriyaki Sauce
1 pound fresh yams or sweet potatoes, peeled and cut into 2-inch chunks
1 large onion, cut into eighths
Hot cooked rice

Cut pork into 1 1/2-inch cubes. Coat in mixture of flour and ginger; reserve 2 tablespoons flour mixture. Heat oil in Dutch oven or large pan; brown pork on all sides in hot oil. Drain pineapple; reserve juice. Add juice, 1 cup water and teriyaki sauce to pork. Cover pan; bring to boil. Reduce heat and simmer 1 hour, stirring occasionally. Add yams to pork; simmer, covered, 10 minutes. Stir in onion; simmer, covered, 20 minutes longer, or until pork and yams are tender. Meanwhile, combine reserved flour mixture and remaining 3/4 cup water; stir into pork mixture and cook until slightly thickened. Stir in pineapple; cook only until heated through. Serve with rice.

GLAZED PORK ROAST

Makes 6 servings

1 (3-pound) boneless pork shoulder roast (Boston butt)
1 cup Kikkoman Teriyaki Sauce
3 tablespoons brown sugar, packed
3 tablespoons dry sherry
1 teaspoon minced fresh ginger root
1 clove garlic, minced
1/4 cup water
2 tablespoons sugar
1 tablespoon cornstarch

MICROWAVE DIRECTIONS:

Pierce meaty parts of roast with fork; place in large plastic bag. Combine teriyaki sauce, brown sugar, sherry, ginger and garlic; pour over roast. Press air out of bag; tie top securely. Refrigerate 8 hours or overnight, turning bag over occasionally. Reserving marinade, remove roast and place, fat side down, in 8×8-inch shallow microwave-safe dish. Brush thoroughly with reserved marinade. Cover roast loosely with waxed paper. Microwave on Medium-high (70%) 30 minutes, or until meat thermometer inserted into thickest part registers 165°F., rotating dish once and brushing with marinade. Remove roast; let stand 10 minutes before slicing. Meanwhile, combine reserved marinade, water, sugar and cornstarch in 2-cup microwave-safe measuring cup. Microwave on High 3 minutes, until mixture boils and thickens, stirring occasionally. Serve teriyaki glaze with roast.

HUNAN STIR-FRY WITH TOFU

Makes 4 servings

- 1 block tofu
- ¹/₂ pound ground pork
- 1 tablespoon dry sherry
- 1 teaspoon minced fresh ginger root
- 1 clove garlic, minced
- ¹/₂ cup regular-strength chicken broth
- 1 tablespoon cornstarch
- 3 tablespoons Kikkoman Soy Sauce
- 1 tablespoon vinegar
- ¹/₂ teaspoon crushed red pepper
- 1 tablespoon vegetable oil
- 1 onion, cut into ³/₄-inch pieces
- 1 green pepper, cut into ³/₄-inch pieces
  Hot cooked rice

Cut tofu into ¹/₂-inch cubes; drain well on several layers of paper towels. Meanwhile, combine pork, sherry, ginger and garlic in small bowl; let stand 10 minutes. Blend broth, cornstarch, soy sauce, vinegar and red pepper; set aside. Heat wok or large skillet over medium-high heat; add pork. Cook, stirring to separate pork, about 3 minutes, or until lightly browned; remove. Heat oil in same pan. Add onion and green pepper; stir-fry 4 minutes. Add pork and soy sauce mixture. Cook and stir until mixture boils and thickens. Gently fold in tofu; heat through. Serve immediately over rice.

Hunan Stir-Fry with Tofu

POULTRY

SPICY CHICKEN

Makes 4 servings

3/4 pound boneless chicken

3 tablespoons Kikkoman Soy Sauce, divided

1 tablespoon cornstarch

1 tablespoon dry sherry

4 teaspoons water

2 tablespoons vegetable oil

1 teaspoon minced fresh ginger root

3/4 teaspoon crushed red pepper

1 small onion, chunked

1 small red or green bell pepper, cut into matchsticks

1 small zucchini, cut into matchsticks

1/2 cup water

Cut chicken into thin slices. Combine chicken and 1 tablespoon soy sauce in small bowl; let stand 30 minutes. Meanwhile, combine remaining 2 tablespoons soy sauce, cornstarch, sherry and 4 teaspoons water. Heat oil in hot wok or large skillet over high heat. Add ginger and crushed red pepper; cook until fragrant. Add chicken and stir-fry 3 minutes. Add onion, bell pepper, zucchini and 1/2 cup water; mix well. Cover and cook 1 minute, or until vegetables are tender-crisp. Add soy sauce mixture; cook and stir until sauce boils and thickens.

SPICY SMOKED DUCK

Makes 4 servings

- 1 (4- to 5-pound) frozen duckling, thawed
- 1/4 cup Kikkoman Lite Soy Sauce
- 1 teaspoon liquid smoke seasoning
- 1/2 teaspoon fennel seed, well crushed
- 1/4 teaspoon pepper
- 1/8 teaspoon ground cloves

Remove and discard giblets and neck from duckling cavity. Wash duckling; drain and gently pat dry with paper towels. Combine lite soy sauce, liquid smoke, fennel, pepper and cloves. Brush body cavity with sauce mixture. Place duckling, breast side up, on rack in roasting pan. Roast at 425°F. 1 hour. *Reduce oven temperature to 350°F.* Continue roasting 45 minutes, or until tender. Brush skin of duckling several times with sauce mixture during last 30 minutes of cooking time. Let stand 15 minutes before carving.

BEIJING CHICKEN

Makes 4 servings

- 3 pounds frying chicken pieces
- 1/2 cup Kikkoman Teriyaki Sauce
- 1 tablespoon dry sherry
- 2 teaspoons minced fresh ginger root
- 1/2 teaspoon fennel seed, crushed
- 1/2 teaspoon grated orange peel
- 1/2 teaspoon honey

Rinse chicken pieces and pat dry with paper towels; place in large plastic bag. Combine teriyaki sauce, sherry, ginger, fennel, orange peel and honey; pour over chicken. Press air out of bag; tie top securely. Refrigerate 8 hours or overnight, turning bag over occasionally. Reserving marinade, remove chicken and place on rack of broiler pan. Broil 5 to 7 inches from heat source about 40 minutes, or until chicken is tender, turning pieces over and basting occasionally with reserved marinade.

MANDARIN CHICKEN SALAD

Makes 4 servings

- 1 whole chicken breast, split
- 2 cups water
- 4 tablespoons Kikkoman Soy Sauce, divided
-   Boiling water
- 3/4 pound fresh bean sprouts
- 1 carrot, peeled and shredded
- 1/2 cup slivered green onions and tops
- 2 tablespoons minced fresh cilantro or parsley
- 1/4 cup distilled white vinegar
- 2 teaspoons sugar
- 1/2 cup blanched slivered almonds, toasted

Simmer chicken in mixture of 2 cups water and 1 tablespoon soy sauce in covered saucepan 15 minutes, or until chicken is tender. Meanwhile, pour boiling water over bean sprouts. Drain; cool under cold water and drain thoroughly. Remove chicken and cool. (Refrigerate stock for another use, if desired.) Skin and bone chicken; shred meat with fingers into large mixing bowl. Add bean sprouts, carrot, green onions and cilantro. Blend vinegar, sugar and remaining 3 tablespoons soy sauce, stirring until sugar dissolves. Pour over chicken and vegetables; toss to coat all ingredients. Cover and refrigerate 1 hour. Just before serving, add almonds and toss to combine.

Spicy Smoked Duck

SICHUAN DRAGON STIR-FRY

Makes 4 servings

- 1 whole chicken breast, skinned and boned
- 1 tablespoon cornstarch
- 4 tablespoons Kikkoman Soy Sauce, divided
- 1/2 teaspoon sugar
- 1 clove garlic, minced
- 1 cup water
- 4 teaspoons cornstarch
- 1/4 to 1/2 teaspoon crushed red pepper
- 2 tablespoons vegetable oil, divided
- 2 carrots, cut diagonally into thin slices
- 1 onion, chunked
- 2 small zucchini, cut in half lengthwise, then diagonally chunked
- 1/4 cup unsalted peanuts
-   Hot cooked rice

Cut chicken into thin, narrow strips. Combine 1 tablespoon *each* cornstarch and soy sauce with sugar and garlic in small bowl; stir in chicken and set aside. Blend water, 4 teaspoons cornstarch, remaining 3 tablespoons soy sauce and red pepper; set aside. Heat 1 tablespoon oil in hot wok or large skillet over high heat. Add chicken and stir-fry 2 minutes; remove. Heat remaining 1 tablespoon oil in same pan. Add carrots and onion; stir-fry 3 minutes. Add zucchini; stir-fry 2 minutes. Add chicken and soy sauce mixture. Cook and stir until sauce boils and thickens. Just before serving, stir in peanuts. Serve immediately with rice.

Cantonese Chicken Salad

CANTONESE CHICKEN SALAD

Makes 6 servings

3 chicken breast halves

2 cups water

5 tablespoons Kikkoman Soy Sauce, divided

4 cups shredded iceberg lettuce

1 medium carrot, peeled and shredded

1/2 cup finely chopped green onions and tops

1/3 cup distilled white vinegar

2 tablespoons sesame seed, toasted

2 teaspoons sugar

1/2 teaspoon ground ginger

2 tablespoons minced fresh cilantro or parsley

Simmer chicken in mixture of water and 1 tablespoon soy sauce in covered saucepan 15 minutes, or until chicken is tender. Remove chicken and cool. (Refrigerate stock for another use, if desired.) Skin and bone chicken; shred meat with fingers into large mixing bowl. Add lettuce, carrot and green onions. Combine vinegar, remaining 4 tablespoons soy sauce, sesame seed, sugar and ginger; stir until sugar dissolves. Pour over chicken and vegetables; toss to coat all ingredients. Cover and refrigerate 1 hour. Just before serving, add cilantro and toss to combine. Garnish as desired.

SHANTUNG CHICKEN

Makes 4 servings

1 whole chicken breast, skinned and boned
2 tablespoons cornstarch, divided
3 tablespoons Kikkoman Soy Sauce, divided
1 tablespoon dry sherry
1 clove garlic, minced
1 cup water
3 tablespoons vegetable oil, divided
1/2 pound fresh bean sprouts
1/4 pound green onions and tops, cut into 1 1/2-inch lengths, separating whites from tops
1 tablespoon slivered fresh ginger root
1 tablespoon sesame seed, toasted
  Hot cooked noodles

Cut chicken into narrow strips. Combine 1 tablespoon *each* cornstarch and soy sauce with sherry and garlic in small bowl; stir in chicken. Let stand 5 minutes. Meanwhile, blend water, remaining 1 tablespoon cornstarch and 2 tablespoons soy sauce; set aside. Heat 1 tablespoon oil in hot wok or large skillet over high heat. Add chicken and stir-fry 2 minutes; remove. Heat remaining 2 tablespoons oil in same pan; add bean sprouts, white parts of green onions and ginger; stir-fry 3 minutes. Stir in chicken, soy sauce mixture, green onion tops and sesame seed. Cook and stir until mixture boils and thickens. Serve immediately over noodles.

Shantung Chicken

Cut chicken into 1-inch square pieces. Remove flowerets from broccoli; cut into bite-size pieces. Peel stalks; cut into thin slices. Heat oil in hot wok or large skillet over high heat. Add chicken; stir-fry 1 minute. Add broccoli and onion; stir-fry 1 minute. Add water; cover and cook 2 minutes, stirring once. Add bell peppers and mushrooms; stir-fry 2 minutes. Stir in stir-fry sauce and crushed red pepper. Cook and stir until chicken and vegetables are coated with sauce. Serve immediately.

THAI HENS

Makes 4 to 6 servings

3 fresh or thawed Rock Cornish hens (1¼ to 1½ pounds each)
½ cup Kikkoman Teriyaki Sauce
1 tablespoon grated lemon peel
1 tablespoon lemon juice
2 cloves garlic, pressed
¼ to ½ teaspoon ground red pepper (cayenne)
1 tablespoon minced fresh cilantro

Remove and discard giblets and necks from hens. Split hens lengthwise. Rinse halves under cold running water; drain well and pat dry with paper towels. Place in large plastic bag. Combine teriyaki sauce, lemon peel and juice, garlic and red pepper; pour over hens. Press air out of bag; tie top securely. Turn bag over several times to coat halves. Refrigerate 8 hours or overnight, turning bag over occasionally. Reserving marinade, remove hens and place on rack of broiler pan. Broil about 7 inches from heat source 45 to 50 minutes, or until tender, turning over frequently and brushing with reserved marinade. Remove to serving platter and immediately sprinkle cilantro over hens.

JADE & RUBY STIR-FRY

Makes 4 servings

1 whole chicken breast, skinned and boned
1 pound fresh broccoli
2 tablespoons vegetable oil
1 medium onion, chunked
2 tablespoons water
2 medium-size red bell peppers, chunked
½ pound fresh mushrooms, quartered
⅓ cup Kikkoman Stir-Fry Sauce
¼ teaspoon crushed red pepper

GOLDEN CHICKEN STIR-FRY

Makes 4 servings

1 whole chicken breast, skinned and boned
1 tablespoon cornstarch
5 tablespoons Kikkoman Teriyaki Sauce, divided
1 clove garlic, minced
1¼ cups regular-strength chicken broth
4 teaspoons cornstarch
Boiling water
½ pound fresh bean sprouts
2 cups finely shredded lettuce
2 tablespoons vegetable oil, divided
2 medium carrots, cut into julienne strips
1 onion, chunked
2 teaspoons slivered fresh ginger root

Cut chicken into thin strips. Combine 1 tablespoon *each* cornstarch and teriyaki sauce with garlic in small bowl; stir in chicken. Let stand 15 minutes. Meanwhile, combine chicken broth, remaining 4 tablespoons teriyaki sauce and 4 teaspoons cornstarch; set aside. Pour boiling water over bean sprouts in bowl; let stand 1 minute. Drain; rinse under cold water and drain thoroughly. Toss sprouts with lettuce. Line serving platter with mixture; set aside. Heat 1 tablespoon oil in hot wok or large skillet over high heat. Add chicken and stir-fry 2 minutes; remove. Heat remaining 1 tablespoon oil in same pan. Add carrots, onion and ginger; stir-fry 4 minutes. Add chicken and teriyaki sauce mixture. Cook and stir until sauce boils and thickens. Turn out onto lined platter; toss to combine before serving.

Golden Chicken Stir-Fry

CHINESE-STYLE POT ROAST CHICKEN

Makes 4 servings

- 3 pounds frying chicken pieces
- 1/4 cup Kikkoman Soy Sauce
- 2 tablespoons vegetable oil
- 1 tablespoon dry sherry
- 1 clove garlic, minced
- 2 stalks celery, cut diagonally into 1/4-inch slices
- 2 green onions and tops, cut into 1-inch lengths
- 3/4 cup water
- 1 tablespoon cornstarch
- 2 tablespoons Kikkoman Soy Sauce
- 1 teaspoon sugar

Rinse chicken pieces and pat dry with paper towels. Rub chicken thoroughly with 1/4 cup soy sauce; let stand 15 minutes. Heat oil in Dutch oven or large skillet over medium heat; add chicken and brown slowly in hot oil. Add sherry and garlic; cover and simmer 30 minutes, or until tender. Remove chicken from pan; keep warm. Add celery and green onions to pan; cook 1 to 2 minutes. Combine water, cornstarch, 2 tablespoons soy sauce and sugar; stir into pan and cook until thickened. Serve sauce and vegetables over chicken.

BRAISED CHINESE DUCKLING

Makes 4 servings

- 1 (4- to 5-pound) frozen duckling, thawed and quartered
- 3 tablespoons Kikkoman Lite Soy Sauce, divided
- 1 tablespoon vegetable oil
- 2 tablespoons dry sherry
- 1 clove garlic, minced
- 1 teaspoon ginger juice*
- 4 green onions and tops, cut into 2-inch lengths
- 1/3 cup water
- 2 teaspoons cornstarch

Wash duckling quarters; dry thoroughly with paper towels. Rub thoroughly with 2 tablespoons lite soy sauce. Let stand 30 minutes. Heat oil in Dutch oven or large skillet over medium heat. Brown duckling slowly in hot oil; drain off fat. Add sherry and garlic. Cover and cook over low heat 45 minutes, or until tender, turning quarters over once. Remove duckling to serving platter; keep warm. Spoon off and discard excess fat from pan juices; return 1/3 cup juices to pan. Add remaining 1 tablespoon lite soy sauce, ginger juice and green onions; cook 1 minute. Combine water with cornstarch; stir into pan. Cook and stir until sauce boils and thickens. To serve, spoon sauce over duckling quarters.

*Peel fresh ginger root, then squeeze through garlic press.

Chinese-Style Pot Roast Chicken

KUNG PAO STIR-FRY

Makes 4 servings

1 whole chicken breast, skinned and boned
2 tablespoons cornstarch, divided
3 tablespoons Kikkoman Teriyaki Sauce, divided
1/4 teaspoon ground red pepper (cayenne)
3/4 cup water
4 teaspoons distilled white vinegar
3/4 pound romaine lettuce
2 tablespoons vegetable oil, divided
1/3 cup roasted peanuts

Cut chicken into thin strips. Combine 1 tablespoon *each* cornstarch and teriyaki sauce with red pepper in small bowl; stir in chicken. Let stand 15 minutes. Meanwhile, combine water, remaining 1 tablespoon cornstarch and 2 tablespoons teriyaki sauce with vinegar; set aside. Separate and rinse lettuce; pat dry. Cut leaves crosswise into 2-inch strips. Heat 1 tablespoon oil in hot wok or large skillet over high heat. Add chicken and stir-fry 2 minutes; remove. Heat remaining 1 tablespoon oil in same pan. Add lettuce; stir-fry 1 minute. Stir in chicken and teriyaki sauce mixture. Cook and stir until mixture boils and thickens. Remove from heat; stir in peanuts. Serve immediately.

ORANGE-CASHEW CHICKEN

Makes 4 servings

1 pound boneless chicken breasts
1/2 cup Kikkoman Teriyaki Baste & Glaze
2 tablespoons orange juice
2 tablespoons dry white wine
2 tablespoons vegetable oil
1 green pepper, cut into thin strips
1/2 cup diagonally sliced celery
1 can (11 oz.) mandarin orange segments, drained
1/2 cup roasted cashews

Cut chicken into thin slices. Combine teriyaki baste & glaze, orange juice and wine; set aside. Heat oil in hot wok or large skillet over medium heat. Add chicken, green pepper and celery; stir-fry 3 to 4 minutes. Pour in baste & glaze mixture; cook and stir until chicken and vegetables are coated with sauce. Remove from heat; stir in orange segments and cashews. Serve immediately.

LOTUS CHICKEN CHOP SUEY

Makes 2 to 3 servings

1/2 chicken breast, skinned and boned
4 tablespoons Kikkoman Teriyaki Sauce, divided
1 cup water
2 tablespoons cornstarch
1 tablespoon dry sherry
1 large carrot, cut diagonally into 1/8-inch slices
1 onion, chunked and separated
1/8 teaspoon salt
1/4 pound fresh bean sprouts
1 package (6 oz.) frozen Chinese pea pods, thawed and drained

MICROWAVE DIRECTIONS:
Cut chicken into narrow strips; place in small bowl. Stir in 2 tablespoons teriyaki sauce; let stand 20 minutes. Meanwhile, blend water, cornstarch, sherry and remaining 2 tablespoons teriyaki sauce in 2-cup microwave-safe measuring cup. Microwave on High 4 minutes, until mixture boils and thickens, stirring occasionally to prevent lumping; set aside. Combine carrot, onion and salt in 2-quart microwave-safe casserole. Microwave, covered, on High 4 minutes, stirring after 2 minutes. Stir in bean sprouts; cover and microwave on High 1 minute. Stir in chicken; microwave, covered, on High 3 minutes, stirring once. Combine cornstarch mixture with chicken and vegetables. Microwave, uncovered, on High 1 minute. Stir in pea pods. Microwave, uncovered, on High 2 minutes, or until mixture is heated through, stirring once.

BRAISED DUCKLING AND PEARS

Makes 3 to 4 servings

1 (4- to 5-pound) frozen duckling, thawed and quartered
1 can (16 oz.) pear halves in heavy syrup
1/3 cup Kikkoman Stir-Fry Sauce
1 cinnamon stick, about 3 inches long

Wash duckling quarters; dry thoroughly with paper towels. Heat large skillet or Dutch oven over medium heat. Add duckling; brown slowly on both sides about 15 minutes, or until golden. Meanwhile, drain pears; reserve all syrup. Remove 1/4 cup pear syrup and combine with stir-fry sauce; set aside. Drain off fat from pan. Pour syrup mixture over duckling; add cinnamon stick. Cover and simmer 40 minutes, or until tender, turning quarters over once. Remove duckling to serving platter; keep warm. Remove and discard cinnamon stick. Pour drippings into measuring cup; skim off fat. Combine 1/2 cup drippings with 2 tablespoons reserved pear syrup; return to pan with pears. Gently bring to boil and cook until pears are heated through, stirring occasionally. Serve duckling with pears and sauce.

ANGEL HAIR STIR-FRY

Makes 4 servings

1 whole chicken breast, skinned and boned
1 tablespoon Kikkoman Stir-Fry Sauce
4 ounces angel hair pasta (capellini)
1/3 cup Kikkoman Stir-Fry Sauce
3 tablespoons water
2 tablespoons vegetable oil, divided
1/4 pound fresh snow peas, cut into julienne strips
1 large carrot, cut into julienne strips
1/8 teaspoon salt
2 teaspoons sesame seed, toasted

Cut chicken into thin strips; coat with 1 tablespoon stir-fry sauce. Let stand 30 minutes. Meanwhile, cook pasta according to package directions, omitting salt. Drain; rinse under cold water and drain thoroughly. Combine 1/3 cup stir-fry sauce and water; set aside. Heat 1 tablespoon oil in hot wok or large skillet over high heat. Add chicken and stir-fry 2 minutes; remove. Heat remaining 1 tablespoon oil in same pan; add peas and carrot. Sprinkle vegetables with salt; stir-fry 4 minutes. Add stir-fry sauce mixture, chicken, pasta and sesame seed. Cook and stir until all ingredients are coated with sauce and pasta is heated through.

CHICKEN ADOBO

Makes 4 servings

3 pounds frying chicken pieces
1/2 cup Kikkoman Soy Sauce
1/2 cup distilled white vinegar
2 tablespoons sugar
1 teaspoon pepper
6 large cloves garlic, pressed

MICROWAVE DIRECTIONS:
Rinse chicken pieces and pat dry with paper towels. Combine soy sauce, vinegar, sugar, pepper and garlic in large microwave-safe casserole with lid; add chicken pieces, skin side down. Cover and microwave on High 10 minutes. Turn chicken pieces over; rearrange in dish. Cover and microwave on High 13 minutes longer, or until chicken is tender, rearranging pieces once. Serve immediately.

Braised Duckling and Pears

COLORFUL DRAGON STIR-FRY

Makes 4 servings

- 1 whole chicken breast, skinned and boned
- 1 pound fresh broccoli
- 5 tablespoons Kikkoman Stir-Fry Sauce, divided
- 3 tablespoons vegetable oil, divided
- 1 medium onion, cut into thin wedges
- 1 medium carrot, cut diagonally into thin slices
- 2 tablespoons water

Cut chicken into ½-inch strips. Remove flowerets from broccoli; set aside. Peel stalks; cut into thin slices. Coat chicken with 1 tablespoon stir-fry sauce. Heat 1 tablespoon oil in hot wok or large skillet over high heat. Add chicken and stir-fry 3 minutes; remove. Heat remaining 2 tablespoons oil in same pan. Add onion; stir-fry 1 minute. Add broccoli and carrot; stir-fry 2 minutes longer. Pour water into pan. Reduce heat and simmer, covered, 3 minutes; stir once. Add remaining 4 tablespoons stir-fry sauce and chicken. Cook and stir just until chicken and vegetables are coated with sauce. Serve immediately.

SHANGHAI TURKEY STIR-FRY

Makes 6 servings

- 1 small turkey thigh, skinned and boned
- 3 tablespoons cornstarch, divided
- 4 tablespoons Kikkoman Soy Sauce, divided
- 1 tablespoon dry sherry
- 1 tablespoon minced fresh ginger root
- 1 clove garlic, minced
- 1 cup water
- 3 tablespoons vegetable oil, divided
- 1 large carrot, cut into julienne strips
- 1 onion, sliced
- 1 package (10 oz.) frozen French-style green beans, thawed and drained

Cut turkey into thin, narrow strips; set aside. Combine 2 tablespoons *each* cornstarch and soy sauce with sherry, ginger and garlic in medium bowl; stir in turkey. Let stand 30 minutes. Meanwhile, combine water, remaining 1 tablespoon cornstarch and 2 tablespoons soy sauce; set aside. Heat 2 tablespoons oil in hot wok or large skillet over high heat. Add turkey and stir-fry 3 minutes, or until tender; remove. Heat remaining 1 tablespoon oil in same pan. Add carrot and onion; stir-fry 2 minutes. Add green beans; stir-fry 1 minute longer. Stir in turkey and soy sauce mixture. Cook and stir until mixture boils and thickens. Serve immediately.

Colorful Dragon Stir-Fry

LETTUCE-WRAPPED PLUM CHICKEN

Makes 8 servings

Orange-Plum Sauce (recipe follows)
1 whole chicken breast, skinned and boned
3 tablespoons Kikkoman Soy Sauce, divided
4 teaspoons cornstarch, divided
1/4 cup water
2 tablespoons vegetable oil, divided
1/2 cup diced carrots
1 cup diced celery
1/2 cup diced onion
1 tablespoon minced fresh ginger root
8 large iceberg lettuce leaves

Prepare Orange-Plum Sauce; cool to room temperature. Meanwhile, dice chicken breast. Combine 1 tablespoon soy sauce and 3 teaspoons cornstarch in small bowl; stir in chicken. Let stand 10 minutes. Combine the remaining 2 tablespoons soy sauce, 1 teaspoon cornstarch and water; set aside. Heat 1 tablespoon oil in hot wok or large skillet over high heat. Add chicken and stir-fry 2 minutes; remove. Heat remaining 1 tablespoon oil in same pan. Add carrots and stir-fry 1 minute. Add celery, onion and ginger; stir-fry 2 minutes longer. Stir in chicken and soy sauce mixture. Cook and stir until mixture boils and thickens. To serve, spread about 2 teaspoons Orange-Plum Sauce in center of each lettuce leaf. Fill each leaf with about 1/4 cup chicken mixture; fold lettuce around filling to enclose.

ORANGE-PLUM SAUCE:
Blend *1/2 cup plum jam, 1/2 teaspoon grated fresh orange peel, 1 pressed garlic clove, 2 tablespoons Kikkoman Teriyaki Sauce, 2 tablespoons orange juice and 1 teaspoon cornstarch* in small saucepan. Bring to boil over medium-high heat; reduce heat and simmer 1 minute, stirring constantly.

MONGOLIAN POT

Makes 4 to 6 servings

2 whole chicken breasts, skinned and boned
4 tablespoons Kikkoman Soy Sauce, divided
2 teaspoons minced fresh ginger root
1/2 teaspoon sugar
2 cans (10 1/4 oz. each) condensed chicken broth
4 soup cans water
1 large clove garlic, minced
1/2 pound cabbage, cut into 3/4-inch chunks (about 4 cups)
3/4 pound fresh spinach, trimmed, washed and drained
3 green onions and tops, cut into 1-inch lengths and slivered
4 ounces vermicelli or thin spaghetti, cooked and drained
1/4 pound fresh mushrooms, sliced

Cut chicken into thin strips. Combine 2 tablespoons soy sauce, ginger and sugar in medium dish; stir in chicken. Let stand 15 minutes. Meanwhile, combine chicken broth, water, remaining 2 tablespoons soy sauce and garlic in deep electric skillet or electric wok; bring to boil. Reduce heat; keep broth mixture hot. Arrange cabbage, spinach, green onions, vermicelli and mushrooms on platter. Using chopsticks or tongs, let individuals select and add chicken, vegetables and vermicelli to hot broth. Cook chicken until tender, vegetables to desired doneness and vermicelli until heated through. Serve in individual bowls with additional soy sauce, as desired. When all foods are cooked, serve broth as soup.

ORIENTAL CHICKEN & CABBAGE SALAD

Makes 4 servings

4 chicken breast halves, skinned and
  boned
2 tablespoons Kikkoman Lite Soy Sauce
2 teaspoons lemon juice
1 teaspoon minced fresh ginger root
1 clove garlic, minced
3 cups shredded cabbage
1 cup shredded carrots
¹/₄ pound fresh bean sprouts
  Lemon-Soy Dressing (recipe follows)

Place chicken in large plastic bag. Combine lite soy sauce, lemon juice, ginger and garlic; pour over chicken. Press air out of bag; tie top securely. Turn over several times to coat pieces well. Marinate 45 minutes, turning bag over occasionally. Meanwhile, combine cabbage, carrots and bean sprouts in large bowl. Prepare Lemon-Soy Dressing. Pour over vegetables; toss well to combine. Cover and refrigerate; toss occasionally. Remove chicken from marinade and place on rack of broiler pan. Broil 5 minutes on each side, or until tender. Slice each breast crosswise into 4 pieces and serve with salad.

LEMON-SOY DRESSING:

Thoroughly combine *2 tablespoons vegetable oil, 2 tablespoons lemon juice, 1 tablespoon Kikkoman Lite Soy Sauce, 1 tablespoon honey, ¹/₂ teaspoon dry mustard and ¹/₄ teaspoon celery seed.*

SPICY CASHEW STIR-FRY

Makes 4 servings

3 chicken breast halves, skinned and
  boned
2 tablespoons vegetable oil
2 teaspoons minced fresh ginger root
6 to 8 whole red chili peppers
1 small onion, thinly sliced
1 small zucchini, thinly sliced
2 tablespoons chicken broth or water
1 tablespoon dry sherry
3 tablespoons Kikkoman Stir-Fry Sauce
¹/₂ cup unsalted roasted cashews

Cut chicken into thin slices. Place wok or large skillet over high heat until hot. Add oil, swirling to coat sides of pan. Add ginger and chili peppers; cook and stir until fragrant. Add chicken and stir-fry 3 minutes. Add onion, zucchini, broth, sherry and stir-fry sauce. Cover; cook 1 minute, or until vegetables are tender-crisp. Stir in cashews; serve immediately.

Chicken Teriyaki Kabobs

CHICKEN TERIYAKI KABOBS

Makes 4 servings

1½ pounds chicken breasts, skinned and boned
1 bunch green onions, cut into 1-inch lengths
½ cup Kikkoman Soy Sauce
2 tablespoons sugar
1 teaspoon vegetable oil
1 teaspoon minced fresh ginger root
1 clove garlic, minced

Cut chicken into 1½-inch square pieces. Thread each of eight 6-inch bamboo or metal skewers alternately with chicken and green onion pieces. (Spear green onion pieces through side.) Place skewers in shallow pan. Combine soy sauce, sugar, oil, ginger and garlic; pour over skewers and brush chicken thoroughly with sauce. Marinate 30 minutes. Reserving marinade, remove skewers and place on rack of broiler pan. Broil 3 minutes; turn over and brush with reserved marinade. Broil 3 minutes longer, or until chicken is tender.

TOMATO & CHICKEN STIR-FRY

Makes 4 servings

¾ pound boneless chicken
4 tablespoons Kikkoman Teriyaki Baste & Glaze, divided
2 tablespoons vegetable oil
1 clove garlic, minced
1 teaspoon minced fresh ginger root
2 medium tomatoes, cut into thin wedges
2 green onions and tops, cut into 2-inch lengths

Cut chicken into thin slices. Combine chicken and 1 tablespoon teriyaki baste & glaze in small bowl; let stand 30 minutes. Heat oil in hot wok or large skillet over high heat. Add garlic and ginger; cook until fragrant. Add chicken and stir-fry 3 minutes. Add tomatoes, green onions and remaining 3 tablespoons teriyaki baste & glaze. Cook and stir about 1 minute to heat through vegetables. Serve immediately.

Hearty Chicken Stir-Fry with Noodles

HEARTY CHICKEN STIR-FRY WITH NOODLES

Makes 4 servings

  1 whole chicken breast, skinned and boned
  1 tablespoon cornstarch
  5 tablespoons Kikkoman Teriyaki Sauce, divided
  1 clove garlic, minced
  1 cup water
  4 teaspoons cornstarch
  2 teaspoons tomato catsup
  2 medium zucchini
  2 cups uncooked fine egg noodles
  2 tablespoons vegetable oil, divided
  1 medium onion, chunked
 10 cherry tomatoes, halved

Cut chicken into 1/2-inch square pieces. Combine 1 tablespoon *each* cornstarch and teriyaki sauce with garlic in small bowl; stir in chicken. Let stand 30 minutes. Meanwhile, combine water, remaining 4 tablespoons teriyaki sauce, 4 teaspoons cornstarch and catsup; set aside. Cut zucchini in half lengthwise, then diagonally into 1-inch pieces. Cook noodles according to package directions; drain and keep warm on serving plate. Heat 1 tablespoon oil in hot wok or large skillet over high heat. Add chicken and stir-fry 2 minutes; remove. Heat remaining 1 tablespoon oil in same pan. Add zucchini and onion; stir-fry 4 minutes. Add chicken, teriyaki sauce mixture and tomatoes. Cook and stir until sauce boils and thickens. Pour over noodles; toss to combine before serving.

CLASSIC SWEET & SOUR CHICKEN

Makes 4 servings

1 whole chicken breast, skinned and boned
1 tablespoon cornstarch
1 tablespoon Kikkoman Soy Sauce
1 teaspoon minced fresh ginger root
1 can (11 oz.) mandarin orange segments
2/3 cup Kikkoman Sweet & Sour Sauce
2 tablespoons vegetable oil, divided
1/2 pound fresh snow peas, trimmed
5 green onions and tops, cut diagonally into thin slices
1/2 cup unsalted roasted peanuts
    Hot cooked rice

Cut chicken into 1-inch pieces. Combine cornstarch, soy sauce and ginger in small bowl; stir in chicken. Let stand 15 minutes. Meanwhile, drain mandarin oranges; reserve 1/4 cup syrup. Blend reserved syrup with sweet & sour sauce; set aside. Heat 1 tablespoon oil in hot wok or large skillet over medium-high heat. Add chicken and stir-fry 2 minutes; remove. Heat remaining 1 tablespoon oil in same pan. Add snow peas; stir-fry 1 minute. Add green onions; stir-fry 30 seconds longer. Add chicken, peanuts and sweet & sour sauce mixture; cook and stir until chicken, vegetables and peanuts are coated with sauce. Gently stir in mandarin oranges; heat through. Serve with rice.

Classic Sweet & Sour Chicken

SEAFOOD

海鮮食譜

SAUCY SHRIMP OVER CHINESE NOODLE CAKES

Makes 4 servings

Chinese Noodle Cakes (recipe follows)
1¼ cups water
2 tablespoons cornstarch, divided
4 tablespoons Kikkoman Soy Sauce, divided
1 teaspoon tomato catsup
½ pound medium-size raw shrimp, peeled and deveined
2 tablespoons vegetable oil, divided
1 clove garlic, minced
½ teaspoon minced fresh ginger root
1 green pepper, chunked
1 medium onion, chunked
2 stalks celery, cut diagonally into thin slices
2 tomatoes, chunked

Prepare Chinese Noodle Cakes on page 76. Combine water, 1 tablespoon cornstarch and 3 tablespoons soy sauce with catsup; set aside. Blend remaining 1 tablespoon cornstarch and 1 tablespoon soy sauce in small bowl; stir in shrimp until coated. Heat 1 tablespoon oil in hot wok or large skillet over high heat. Add shrimp and stir-fry 1 minute; remove. Heat remaining 1 tablespoon oil in same pan. Add garlic and ginger; stir-fry until fragrant. Add green pepper, onion and celery; stir-fry 4 minutes. Stir in soy sauce mixture, shrimp and tomatoes. Cook and stir until sauce boils and thickens. Cut Chinese Noodle Cakes into squares and serve with shrimp mixture.

CHINESE NOODLE CAKES:

Cook *8 ounces capellini (angel hair pasta)* according to package directions. Drain; rinse under cold water and drain thoroughly. Heat *1 tablespoon vegetable oil* in large, nonstick skillet over medium-high heat. Add half the capellini; slightly spread to fill bottom of skillet to form noodle cake. Without stirring, cook 5 minutes, or until golden on bottom. Lift cake with wide spatula; add *1 tablespoon oil* to skillet and turn cake over. Cook 5 minutes longer, or until golden brown, shaking skillet occasionally to brown evenly; remove to rack and keep warm in 200°F. oven. Repeat with remaining capellini.

CHINESE PORCUPINE MEATBALLS

Makes 4 servings

- 1/2 cup uncooked rice
- 6 ounces medium-size raw shrimp
- 1 pound ground pork
- 2/3 cup chopped green onions and tops
- 3 tablespoons Kikkoman Soy Sauce
- 1 tablespoon dry sherry
- 2 cloves garlic, pressed
  Mandarin Peach Sauce (see page 54)

Cover rice with warm water and let stand 20 minutes; drain. Meanwhile, peel, devein and mince shrimp. Combine shrimp with pork, green onions, soy sauce, sherry, garlic and rice; mix well. Divide into 8 equal portions; shape portions into meatballs. Arrange meatballs on steamer rack. Set rack in large saucepan or wok of boiling water. (Do not allow water level to reach meatballs.) Cover and steam 45 minutes, or until meatballs are cooked. Serve with warm Mandarin Peach Sauce.

SHANGHAI SWEET & SOUR FISH

Makes 4 servings

- 1 cup water
- 1/4 cup brown sugar, packed
- 1/4 cup orange juice
- 2 1/2 tablespoons cornstarch
- 3 tablespoons Kikkoman Lite Soy Sauce
- 3 tablespoons vinegar
- 1 tablespoon tomato catsup
- 2 teaspoons minced fresh ginger root
- 1 large onion, chunked and separated
- 1 large green pepper, chunked
- 1 large carrot, sliced diagonally into very thin slices
- 1 pound firm fish fillets (swordfish, halibut, mahi-mahi, shark), 3/4 inch thick

MICROWAVE DIRECTIONS:

Combine water, brown sugar, orange juice, cornstarch, lite soy sauce, vinegar, catsup and ginger; set aside. Combine onion, green pepper and carrot in large microwave-safe casserole. Cover and microwave on High 4 minutes. Stir in soy sauce mixture; cover and microwave on High 4 minutes. Remove from oven and let stand, covered, about 5 minutes. Meanwhile, cut fish into 1-inch pieces and place in single layer in separate small microwave-safe casserole. Cover and microwave on Medium-high (70%) 4 to 5 minutes, or until fish flakes easily when tested with fork, rotating dish once. Remove fish and add to vegetable mixture, stirring gently to combine. Serve immediately.

Chinese Porcupine Meatballs

Grilled Oriental Fish Steaks

GINGER FISH FILLETS

Makes 4 servings

1 pound fresh or thawed fish fillets
1/4 cup Kikkoman Teriyaki Sauce
1 tablespoon vegetable oil
1 teaspoon sugar
1 tablespoon slivered fresh ginger root
1 large green onion and top, cut into
    1-inch lengths and slivered
1/3 cup water
1 1/2 teaspoons cornstarch

Place fillets in single layer in shallow baking pan. Combine teriyaki sauce, oil and sugar; pour over fish. Turn fillets over to coat well. Marinate 20 minutes, turning fish over occasionally. (If fillets are very thin, marinate for only 10 minutes.) Sprinkle ginger and green onion evenly over each fillet. Bake in marinade at 350°F. 6 to 10 minutes, or until fish flakes easily when tested with fork. Remove to serving platter and keep warm; reserve 1/4 cup pan juices. Blend water and cornstarch in small saucepan. Stir in reserved pan juices. Cook and stir until mixture boils and thickens. To serve, spoon sauce over fish.

GRILLED ORIENTAL FISH STEAKS

Makes 4 servings

4 fish steaks (halibut, salmon or
    swordfish), about 3/4 inch thick
1/4 cup Kikkoman Lite Soy Sauce
3 tablespoons minced onion
1 tablespoon chopped fresh ginger root
1 tablespoon sesame seed, toasted
1/2 teaspoon sugar

Place fish in single layer in shallow baking pan. Measure lite soy sauce, onion, ginger, sesame seed and sugar into blender container; process on low speed 30 seconds, scraping sides down once. Pour sauce over fish; turn over to coat both sides. Marinate 30 minutes, turning fish over occasionally. Remove fish and broil or grill 4 inches from heat source or moderately hot coals 5 minutes on each side, or until fish flakes easily when tested with fork. Garnish as desired.

TERIYAKI TROUT

Makes 4 servings

4 medium trout (about 2 pounds),
   dressed
1/2 cup Kikkoman Teriyaki Sauce
1/4 teaspoon grated lemon peel
3 tablespoons lemon juice
4 teaspoons Kikkoman Teriyaki Sauce

Score both sides of trout with diagonal slashes
1/4 inch deep and 1 inch apart; place in large
shallow pan. Pour 1/2 cup teriyaki sauce over
trout, turning over to coat both sides well.
Cover and refrigerate 1 hour, turning over
once. Meanwhile, combine lemon peel and
juice and 4 teaspoons teriyaki sauce; set aside.
Reserving marinade, remove trout and place
on rack of broiler pan. Broil 3 inches from heat
source, 5 minutes on each side, or until fish
flakes easily when tested with fork; brush occasionally with reserved marinade. Serve with
lemon-teriyaki sauce.

ORIENTAL STEAMED FISH

Makes 4 servings

4 white fish steaks, about 3/4 inch thick
1 tablespoon slivered fresh ginger root
1/4 cup orange juice
2 tablespoons Kikkoman Soy Sauce
1 1/2 teaspoons distilled white vinegar
1/2 teaspoon brown sugar
1 teaspoon Oriental sesame oil
2 green onions and tops, minced

Place fish, in single layer, on oiled rack of bamboo steamer; sprinkle ginger evenly over fish.
Set rack in large pot or wok of boiling water.
(Do not allow water level to reach fish.) Cover
and steam 8 to 10 minutes, or until fish flakes
easily when tested with fork. Meanwhile, combine orange juice, soy sauce, vinegar and
brown sugar in small saucepan; bring to boil.
Remove from heat; stir in sesame oil. Arrange
fish on serving platter; sprinkle green onions
over fish and pour sauce over all.

IMPERIAL SESAME FISH

Makes 4 to 6 servings

2 teaspoons sesame seed, toasted
1/4 cup Kikkoman Soy Sauce
2 teaspoons distilled white vinegar
2 teaspoons minced fresh ginger root
1/2 teaspoon sugar
1/2 cup water
1 1/2 pounds fresh or thawed fish fillets,
    1/2 to 3/4 inch thick
2 teaspoons cornstarch
1 green onion and top, chopped

Measure sesame seed into blender container; cover and process about 10 seconds, or until finely ground. Add soy sauce, vinegar, ginger and sugar; cover and process about 15 seconds, scraping down sides once. Remove 3 tablespoons sauce mixture from blender container; combine with water in small saucepan and set aside. Generously brush both sides of fish with remaining sauce. Broil about 5 minutes, or until fish flakes easily when tested with fork. Meanwhile, blend cornstarch with mixture in saucepan. Bring to boil; cook and stir until sauce thickens. Stir in green onion. Just before serving, spoon sauce over cooked fish. Serve with assorted vegetables.

Teriyaki Trout

SICHUAN SQUID STIR-FRY

Makes 4 servings

1 pound fresh or thawed medium squid
    Boiling water
2 tablespoons cornstarch, divided
4 tablespoons Kikkoman Teriyaki Sauce,
    divided
3/4 cup water
1/8 to 1/4 teaspoon crushed red pepper
2 tablespoons vegetable oil, divided
1 red bell pepper, cut into 1/4-inch strips
1/4 pound green onions and tops, cut into
    2-inch lengths, separating whites
    from tops
1 tablespoon minced fresh ginger root
1 clove garlic, minced
3 cups shredded iceberg lettuce

Clean, skin and wash squid.* Cut body sacs into 1/4-inch rings; place in bowl with tentacles. Add enough boiling water to cover; let stand 3 minutes. Drain; cool under cold water and drain thoroughly. Spread on paper towels and blot dry. Combine 1 tablespoon *each* cornstarch and teriyaki sauce in medium bowl; stir in squid. Let stand 10 minutes. Meanwhile, combine water, remaining 1 tablespoon cornstarch, 3 tablespoons teriyaki sauce and crushed red pepper; set aside. Heat 1 tablespoon oil in hot wok or large skillet over medium-high heat. Add squid and stir-fry 2 minutes; remove. Heat remaining 1 tablespoon oil in same pan. Add red bell pepper, white parts of green onions, ginger and garlic; stir-fry 2 minutes. Stir in squid, lettuce, green onion tops and teriyaki sauce mixture. Cook and stir until mixture boils and thickens. Serve immediately.

*To clean squid, carefully pull heads from body sacs; discard viscera. Set aside heads with tentacles. Remove transparent quill from inside sacs; wash insides thoroughly to remove all matter. Pull off speckled outer skin covering sacs. Cut tentacles from heads; discard hard "beaks" and heads.

SHANGHAI SHRIMP STIR-FRY

Makes 4 servings

- 2 tablespoons cornstarch, divided
- 3 tablespoons Kikkoman Soy Sauce, divided
- 1 tablespoon minced fresh ginger root
- 1/2 teaspoon sugar
- 1/2 pound medium-size raw shrimp, peeled and deveined
- 1 1/4 cups water
- 1/4 teaspoon fennel seed, crushed
- 1/8 teaspoon ground cloves
- 1/8 teaspoon pepper
- 1 pound fresh broccoli
- 3 tablespoons vegetable oil, divided
- 1 onion, chunked and separated

Combine 1 tablespoon *each* cornstarch and soy sauce with ginger and sugar in small bowl; stir in shrimp. Let stand 10 minutes. Meanwhile, combine water, remaining 1 tablespoon cornstarch and 2 tablespoons soy sauce, fennel, cloves and pepper; set aside. Remove flowerets from broccoli; cut into bite-size pieces. Peel stalks; cut into thin slices. Heat 1 tablespoon oil in hot wok or large skillet over high heat. Add shrimp and stir-fry 1 minute; remove. Heat remaining 2 tablespoons oil in same pan. Add broccoli; stir-fry 2 minutes. Add onion; stir-fry 3 minutes longer. Stir in shrimp and soy sauce mixture; cook and stir until sauce boils and thickens.

SEA BREEZE FISH SALAD

Makes 4 servings

- 1 pound firm white fish fillets (red snapper, sea bass or orange roughy), about 1 inch thick
- 1 3/4 cups water
- 1 tablespoon grated lemon peel
- 6 tablespoons lemon juice, divided
- 3 tablespoons Kikkoman Lite Soy Sauce, divided
- 6 ounces fresh snow peas, trimmed and cut diagonally into 1-inch pieces
- 2 tablespoons vegetable oil
- 1 tablespoon minced onion
- 1/2 teaspoon thyme, crumbled
- 1/4 teaspoon sugar
- 1/2 medium cantaloupe, chunked
- 1 tablespoon minced fresh cilantro or parsley

Cut fish into 1-inch cubes. Combine water, lemon peel, 4 tablespoons lemon juice and 1 tablespoon lite soy sauce in large skillet. Heat only until mixture starts to simmer. Add fish; simmer, uncovered, 3 minutes, or until fish flakes easily when tested with fork. Remove fish with slotted spoon to plate. Cool slightly; cover and refrigerate 1 hour, or until thoroughly chilled. Meanwhile, cook snow peas in boiling water 2 minutes, or until tender-crisp; cool under cold water and drain thoroughly. Chill. Measure remaining 2 tablespoons lemon juice and 2 tablespoons lite soy sauce, oil, onion, thyme and sugar into jar with screw-top lid; cover and shake well. Combine peas, cantaloupe and cilantro in large bowl; add dressing and toss to coat all ingredients. Add fish and gently stir to combine. Serve immediately.

Sea Breeze Fish Salad

CALIFORNIA SUSHI

Makes 4 to 6 servings

- 1 large head iceberg lettuce
- 1½ cups uncooked long-grain rice, washed and drained
- 2 cups water
- ¼ cup distilled white vinegar
- 3 tablespoons sugar
- 2 teaspoons salt
- ½ pound crabmeat or imitation crabmeat
- 2 large ripe avocados
  Kikkoman Soy Sauce

Core, rinse and thoroughly drain lettuce; refrigerate in plastic bag. Combine rice and water in medium saucepan; bring to boil. Reduce heat and simmer, covered, 20 minutes, or until water is absorbed. Remove from heat and let stand, covered, 20 minutes. Meanwhile, combine vinegar, sugar and salt in small saucepan. Cook over low heat only until sugar dissolves, stirring constantly. Turn out cooked rice into large nonmetal bowl, separating grains with fork. Pour vinegar mixture, a little at a time, evenly over rice; gently fold in to combine after each addition. Cool rice mixture to room temperature. Cut lettuce head in half lengthwise. Carefully separate leaves; set aside. Cut or shred crabmeat into bite-size strips. Just before serving, cut each avocado in half; remove seed and peel. Cut each half lengthwise into 8 thin slices. Arrange avocado slices, lettuce leaves and crabmeat on large platter. Fluff rice mixture with fork. To serve, place lettuce leaf in palm of hand. Spread 1 to 2 tablespoonfuls rice mixture in center of lettuce. Top with 1 avocado slice and small amount of crabmeat. Wrap lettuce around filling in cone shape to enclose. Serve with soy sauce.

California Sushi

Shrimp-in-Shell

SHRIMP-IN-SHELL

Makes 4 to 6 servings

1 pound medium-size raw shrimp,
  unpeeled
1/2 cup regular-strength chicken broth
2 tablespoons cornstarch
3 tablespoons Kikkoman Soy Sauce
2 teaspoons sugar
3 tablespoons vegetable oil
1 tablespoon minced fresh ginger root
1 large clove garlic, minced
1 red bell pepper, cut into thin strips
1/4 pound fresh snow peas, trimmed

Thoroughly rinse shrimp; devein. Let drain on
several layers of paper towels. Combine
chicken broth, cornstarch, soy sauce and
sugar; set aside. Heat oil in hot wok or large
skillet over high heat. Add ginger and garlic;
stir-fry 30 seconds. Add shrimp; stir-fry 1 to 2
minutes, or until pink. Remove shrimp with
slotted spoon, leaving oil in pan. Add red pepper and snow peas to same pan; stir-fry 1 minute. Stir in shrimp and soy sauce mixture.
Cook and stir until mixture boils and thickens,
about 1 minute.

EMPEROR'S SWEET &
SOUR FISH

Makes 4 to 6 servings

1 1/2 pounds fresh or thawed fish fillets,
  1/2 inch thick
1 can (6 oz.) unsweetened pineapple juice
1/4 cup Kikkoman Soy Sauce
1/4 cup water
1/4 cup sugar
2 tablespoons cornstarch
3 tablespoons vinegar
2 tablespoons tomato catsup
  Dash ground red pepper (cayenne)
1/4 cup minced green onions and tops

MICROWAVE DIRECTIONS:
Place fish in single layer in large microwave-
safe dish; set aside. Combine pineapple juice,
soy sauce, water, sugar, cornstarch, vinegar,
catsup and red pepper in 2-cup microwave-safe
measuring cup. Microwave on High 5 minutes,
or until mixture boils and thickens, stirring occasionally to prevent lumping. Remove 1/4 cup
sauce and pour over fillets, turning each piece
over to coat both sides. Keep remaining sauce
warm. Cover fish with waxed paper; microwave
on High 8 minutes, or until fish flakes easily
when tested with fork, turning dish once. Remove fillets to serving platter with slotted
spoon. To serve, drizzle warm sauce over fillets
and sprinkle green onions over sauce. Pass remaining sauce.

SIDE DISHES

JAPANESE RICE SALAD

Makes 6 servings

2 cups water
3 tablespoons Kikkoman Lite Soy Sauce, divided
1 cup uncooked long-grain rice, washed and
  drained
1/2 pound cooked baby shrimp
1 carrot, peeled and shredded
1/2 cup frozen green peas, thawed and drained
1/2 cup chopped green onions and tops
1 tablespoon minced fresh ginger root
1/4 cup distilled white vinegar
2 tablespoons sugar
2 teaspoons sesame seed, toasted
2 teaspoons water
  Lettuce leaves

Combine 2 cups water and 2 tablespoons lite soy sauce in medium saucepan. Bring to boil; stir in rice. Reduce heat and simmer, covered, 20 minutes, or until water is absorbed. Remove from heat and cool in pan. Rinse shrimp; drain thoroughly. Remove and reserve 1/2 cup. Combine remaining shrimp, carrot, peas, green onions and ginger in large bowl. Fluff rice with fork; fold into shrimp mixture. Cover and refrigerate until chilled. Meanwhile, measure vinegar, sugar, remaining 1 tablespoon lite soy sauce, sesame seed and 2 teaspoons water into jar with screw-top lid. Cover and shake until blended and sugar dissolves. Pour over rice mixture; toss to coat all ingredients well. Spoon over lettuce leaves on serving plates; sprinkle with reserved shrimp. Garnish as desired.

ORIENTAL TOSS

Makes 6 servings

Boiling water
1/4 pound fresh snow peas, trimmed
1/4 pound fresh bean sprouts
1 head curly leaf lettuce, washed and drained
1/4 pound fresh mushrooms, sliced
1/4 cup distilled white vinegar
2 tablespoons sugar
2 tablespoons Kikkoman Soy Sauce
2 tablespoons water
1/2 teaspoon ground ginger

Pour enough boiling water over snow peas in small bowl to cover; let stand 10 minutes. Drain; cool under cold water and drain thoroughly. Pour boiling water over bean sprouts in colander; cool immediately under cold water and drain thoroughly. Tear lettuce into bite-size pieces; combine with snow peas, bean sprouts and mushrooms in large serving bowl. Cover and refrigerate until chilled. Meanwhile, combine vinegar, sugar, soy sauce, water and ginger until sugar dissolves. Pour desired amount of dressing over salad mixture; toss well to coat all ingredients.

HOT & SPICY GLAZED CARROTS

Makes 4 servings

2 tablespoons vegetable oil
2 dried red chili peppers
1 pound carrots, peeled and cut diagonally into 1/8-inch slices
1/4 cup Kikkoman Teriyaki Baste & Glaze

Heat oil in hot wok or large skillet over high heat. Add peppers and stir-fry until darkened; remove and discard. Add carrots; reduce heat to medium. Stir-fry 4 minutes, or until tender-crisp. Stir in teriyaki baste & glaze and cook until carrots are glazed. Serve immediately.

CUCUMBER FAN SALAD

Makes 6 servings

2 large cucumbers
1 teaspoon salt
1 teaspoon sesame seed
2 tablespoons vegetable oil
1/8 teaspoon ground red pepper (cayenne)
1/4 cup distilled white vinegar
2 tablespoons sugar
1 tablespoon Kikkoman Soy Sauce

Trim off and discard ends of cucumbers, then peel lengthwise with vegetable peeler to form stripes. Cut each cucumber in half lengthwise; remove seeds. Slice each half crosswise into 1-inch pieces. Score each piece crosswise, making cuts close together to within 1/4 inch of edges. Place cucumbers in large bowl and sprinkle evenly with salt; let stand 30 minutes, tossing occasionally. Meanwhile, toast sesame seed in small dry skillet over medium-high heat. Remove from heat and stir in oil and red pepper; cool. Blend vinegar, sugar and soy sauce; stir into sesame seed mixture. Rinse cucumbers. Drain and pat dry; return to bowl. Pour dressing over cucumbers and toss to coat well. Cover and refrigerate 1 hour, stirring occasionally. Remove cucumbers from dressing. Gently spread each piece to form a fan and arrange on serving dish.

Top: Oriental Toss
Bottom: Hot & Spicy Glazed Carrots

Sprout-Cucumber Salad

SPROUT-CUCUMBER SALAD

Makes 8 servings

Boiling water
1 pound fresh bean sprouts
1 medium cucumber, thinly sliced
¼ cup finely chopped green onions and tops
2 tablespoons distilled white vinegar
2 tablespoons Kikkoman Soy Sauce
2 tablespoons vegetable oil
1¼ teaspoons sugar
1 tablespoon sesame seed, toasted (optional)

Pour boiling water over bean sprouts in colander; rinse immediately with cold water. Drain thoroughly. Arrange cucumber slices around outer edge of serving plate; set aside. Toss green onions with sprouts. Measure vinegar, soy sauce, oil and sugar in jar with screw-top lid; cover and shake well. Toss sprout mixture with about ⅔ of the dressing until thoroughly coated. Drizzle remaining dressing over cucumbers. Spoon sprout mixture in center of serving plate; sprinkle sesame seed over all. Serve immediately.

ORIENTAL TEA EGGS

Makes 8 eggs

8 tea bags or 3 tablespoons loose black
   tea leaves
3 cups water
1/2 cup Kikkoman Teriyaki Sauce
8 eggs, room temperature

Combine tea bags, water and teriyaki sauce in medium saucepan; add eggs. Bring to full boil over high heat. Remove from heat; cover tightly and let stand 10 minutes. Remove eggs; reserve liquid. Place eggs under cold running water until cool enough to handle. Gently tap each eggshell with back of metal spoon until eggs are covered with fine cracks *(do not peel eggs)*. Return eggs to reserved liquid. Bring to boil; reduce heat, cover and simmer 25 minutes. Drain off liquid and refrigerate eggs until chilled, about 1 hour. Peel carefully before serving.

SAVORY LUAU RICE

Makes 8 to 10 servings

1/4 cup butter or margarine
2 cups uncooked white rice
3 1/2 cups water
1/2 cup Kikkoman Soy Sauce
1/2 cup chopped green onions and tops

Melt butter in 2-quart saucepan; stir in rice until well coated. Add water and soy sauce; bring to boil. Cover; reduce heat and simmer 30 minutes, or until liquid is absorbed. Remove from heat and let stand, covered, 20 minutes. Before serving, stir in green onions.

CHICKEN FRIED RICE

Makes 6 to 8 servings

1/2 pound boneless, skinless chicken
   breast
2 tablespoons vegetable oil
3 green onions and tops, chopped
1 carrot, cut into julienne strips
1 egg, beaten
4 cups cold, cooked rice
3 tablespoons Kikkoman Soy Sauce

Cut chicken into thin strips. Heat oil in hot wok or large skillet over high heat. Add chicken, green onions and carrot. Stir-fry 3 minutes, or until chicken is browned and carrot is tender-crisp. Add egg; cook, stirring gently, until firm. Stir in rice and cook until heated through, gently separating grains. Add soy sauce and stir until mixture is well blended.

Oriental Tea Eggs

HUNAN-STYLE STUFFED CUCUMBERS

Makes 4 to 6 servings

3 cucumbers, each about 6 inches long
$^1/_4$ pound medium-size raw shrimp, peeled and deveined
$^3/_4$ pound ground pork
2 tablespoons Kikkoman Soy Sauce
2 tablespoons finely chopped green onions and tops
$^1/_4$ to $^1/_2$ teaspoon crushed red pepper
1 clove garlic, pressed

Trim off and discard ends of cucumbers, then peel lengthwise with vegetable peeler to form stripes. Cut each cucumber crosswise into 1$^1/_2$-inch lengths. Scoop out and discard seeds and enough flesh to make about $^1/_4$-inch shell on sides and bottoms; set aside. Mince shrimp; combine with pork, soy sauce, green onions, red pepper and garlic. Stuff cucumber shells evenly with mixture; place on steamer rack. Set rack in large pot or wok of boiling water. (Do not allow water level to reach cucumbers.) Cover and steam 12 to 15 minutes, or until pork is cooked.

Hunan-Style Stuffed Cucumbers

EAST MEETS WEST SALAD

Makes 6 to 8 servings

6 cups shredded iceberg lettuce
1 large carrot, peeled and shredded
1 tablespoon minced fresh cilantro or parsley
2 tablespoons distilled white vinegar
4 teaspoons Kikkoman Soy Sauce
1 tablespoon sesame seed, toasted
1 tablespoon water
2 teaspoons sugar

Toss lettuce with carrot and cilantro. Measure vinegar, soy sauce, sesame seed, water and sugar into jar with screw-top lid; cover and shake well until sugar dissolves. Pour over lettuce mixture and toss lightly to combine. Serve immediately.

East Meets West Salad

PAGODA FRIED RICE

Makes 6 servings

2 strips bacon, cut crosswise into ¼-inch-wide pieces
6 green onions and tops, thinly sliced
1 egg, beaten
4 cups cold, cooked rice
2 tablespoons Kikkoman Soy Sauce

Cook bacon in hot wok or large skillet over medium heat until crisp. Add green onions and stir-fry 1 minute. Add egg and scramble. Stir in rice and cook until heated through, gently separating grains. Add soy sauce and stir until mixture is well blended.

HOT ORIENTAL SALAD

Makes 6 to 8 servings

1 small head napa (Chinese cabbage)
¾ pound fresh spinach
1 tablespoon vegetable oil
2 cloves garlic, minced
½ teaspoon ground ginger
2 stalks celery, cut into julienne strips
½ pound fresh mushrooms, sliced
2 tablespoons Kikkoman Soy Sauce

Separate and rinse napa; pat dry. Slice enough leaves crosswise into 1-inch pieces to measure 8 cups. Wash and drain spinach; tear into pieces. Heat oil in Dutch oven over medium-high heat; add garlic and ginger. Stir-fry until garlic is lightly browned. Add celery; stir-fry 2 minutes. Add cabbage and mushrooms; stir-fry 2 minutes. Add spinach; stir-fry 2 minutes longer. Stir in soy sauce; serve immediately.

SHRIMP FRIED RICE

Makes 6 servings

2 eggs
2 tablespoons water
2 tablespoons vegetable oil
3 green onions and tops, chopped
3 cups cold, cooked rice
¼ pound cooked baby shrimp, chopped
3 tablespoons Kikkoman Soy Sauce

Beat eggs with water just to blend; set aside. Heat oil in hot wok or large skillet over medium heat. Add green onions; stir-fry 30 seconds. Add eggs and scramble. Stir in rice and cook until heated, gently separating grains. Add shrimp and soy sauce; cook and stir until heated through. Serve immediately.

Firecracker Salad

FIRECRACKER SALAD

Makes 6 servings

1 tablespoon sesame seed, toasted
2 tablespoons distilled white vinegar
2 teaspoons sugar
1 teaspoon minced fresh ginger root
4 teaspoons Kikkoman Soy Sauce
1 cup julienne-stripped radishes
1 cup julienne-stripped cucumber
4 cups finely shredded iceberg lettuce
1½ teaspoons minced fresh cilantro or parsley

Measure sesame seed, vinegar, sugar, ginger and soy sauce into jar with screw-top lid; cover and shake well until sugar dissolves. Combine radishes, cucumber and 3 tablespoons dressing; cover and refrigerate 30 minutes, stirring occasionally. Toss lettuce with cilantro in large bowl. Pour radish mixture and remaining dressing over lettuce. Toss lightly to combine.

HALEAKALA RICE

Makes 6 servings

1 can (20 oz.) crushed pineapple in syrup
2 tablespoons butter or margarine
1 cup uncooked white rice
2 tablespoons chopped parsley
2 tablespoons Kikkoman Soy Sauce
1 teaspoon dried mint
2 tablespoons freeze-dried chopped chives

Drain pineapple well; reserve syrup. Melt butter in 2-quart saucepan; stir in rice until well coated. Add enough water to reserved pineapple syrup to measure 2 cups; stir into rice. Add parsley, soy sauce and mint; bring to boil. Cover; reduce heat and simmer 35 to 40 minutes, or until liquid is absorbed. Remove from heat; stir in pineapple and chives.

INDEX